Penguin Education
Penguin Education Specials
General Editor: Willem van der Eyken

Learner Teacher
Nicholas Otty

Learner Teacher
Nicholas Otty

RXTSA

Penguin Books

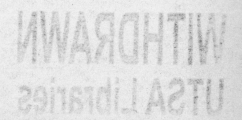

Penguin Books Ltd, Harmondsworth,
Middlesex, England
Penguin Books Inc, 7110 Ambassador Road,
Baltimore, Md 21207, USA
Penguin Books Australia Ltd,
Ringwood, Victoria, Australia

First published 1972
Copyright © Nicholas Otty, 1972

Made and printed in Great Britain by
Cox & Wyman Ltd, London, Reading and Fakenham
Set in Intertype Plantin

For Sue

Contents

Part One
The Institute

Autumn term

Why do I feel so irritated by this University? They keep on telling us that the post-graduate education year will give us a chance to 're-examine our basic assumptions' . . . which is pretty patronizing. How do they know I don't spend all my time agonizing over my basic assumptions? Why after all did I come here?

Well, why?

It was not quite the normal course of events, I suppose. At Cambridge the people I knew who decided to stay on and do the post-graduate certificate gave various reasons which were nothing to do with education: another season of Cambridge cricket, or a girl friend who still had a year to do at Homerton.

I had decided to go abroad, and the easiest way of doing that with an English degree was to go and teach English. So I spent a year at an iniquitous establishment in Switzerland designed to fleece the rich of Germany, Austria, England and America. I had to prepare the pupils for exams in literature which included questions like this:

(a) A thing of beauty is a joy for ever:
(b) Its loveliness increases; it will never
(c) Pass into nothingness; but still will keep
(d) A bower quiet for us, and a sleep
(e) Full of sweet dreams, and health and quiet breathing.

Which is the best of these five lines? Place the letter indicating the line you select in the box provided ☐.

The job gave me time, and distance, however, to think about private schools and to wonder about the British state system of education. My own memories of the latter are of a brief time in a Scottish kindergarten. I remember playing with bricks and sand and seeing the tawse being used on the junior-school pupils.

When I returned to England after a year, I found that the state-school headmasters regarded me as rather suspect. Why had I gone to Switzerland? Why not get down to my chosen profession straight away? And so on. I *was* offered a job in a dismal commuter-belt grammar school. I was asked only one question about English teaching at the interview . . .

'Mr Otty,' said the head, 'how would you help a child who could not spell?'

My reply was very vague, and the head promptly offered me a twenty-minute lecture on the subject – something to do with Pavlov, I think. But I couldn't face that place so I opted for a crammer near the British Museum.

It was an old-established firm and I think it must have originally offered the sons of gentlemen a second go at the Sandhurst entry. But when I joined its staff it had two functions. One was to pick up and set on their feet again all kinds of drop-outs from state schools, public schools, progressive schools and so on. The other was to give basic 'O' and 'A' level qualifications to aspiring barristers from Nigeria, Malaya, Sierra Leone, Trinidad, Hong Kong . . . from China to Peru. One's classes, therefore, were a bizarre and stimulating mixture, and the job was not without its problems. How do you deal with a practice 'O' level comprehension test about frozen canals and locks in a snow-covered Wigan, when half your class do not know what a canal is, and a third have never seen snow? To explain locks requires a course in nineteenth-century hydraulic engineering – then one has to start explaining slagheaps. On one occasion we were doing a comprehension on hunting – another wintry descriptive passage as I remember.

'Mr Otty, why should they wear pink coats?'

'Well, they're not pink, actually. They're scarlet.' I am being interrogated by an interested but puzzled Sierra Leonian.

'Is it a kind of camouflage?'

'No, it's a kind of tradition.'

Someone else takes over the questioning.

'What is this fox?'

'A small reddish furry animal with a bushy tail.'

'It is good to eat?'

'No.'

'They must keep *part* of it surely?'

'The paws, the head, and. . . .' I can see they don't believe me . . . 'and the bushy tail.'

I can remember they laughed quite a lot at that. But it did throw into relief the fact that learning a language is learning a culture – a whole way of life. Simply practising comprehension exercises was not going to get this lot anywhere. After all the work we did on Wigan and fox-hunting, they might well get a passage in the exam on cocktail parties, or children's comics, or Morris dancing.

So after two years of that kind of problem I have come to the Institute.

Why?

To see what the professionals have to say about English teaching? To make myself educationally respectable again by taking another exam? Something of both. Why *does* one choose to do something?

Anyway, here I am. And we have sat in a gigantic, faded, luxury cinema of a lecture hall, and we have been abused about our basic assumptions. And we have been told we are in for an 'orientation period' with coy jokes about it being more of a disorientation period.

The staff of the Institute are democratic to the point of vulgarity. And this fact is in strange contrast to the architecture which is fascist, or totalitarian in inspiration. It is a massive, pyramidal, pseudo skyscraper. 'Pseudo' because although it is huge, it is not as big as it looks. The windows of the central tower are reduced in size in the upper floors to give an impression of distance. As you approach the main entrance at the base of this tower you feel like an ant with its flies undone. What is worse is that after a bit you feel that the building was designed as the central feature of a massive military rally. There should be a tiny saluting figure on the balcony above the entrance; there should be tannoys and bands and flags and guns. All the elegant Georgian squares and streets surrounding this monstrosity should be flattened and tarmaced to accommodate an army of cheering heads.

But this is only an accident of its date. Of course, inside the bizarre exterior nestles a haven of rational inquiry and selfless study . . .

Inside the shell, however, the architect gave up. The windows, positioned for external effect, are a failure as far as lighting the interior goes. Sometimes the sill of the window is a yard above your head, as you stand in a dim dusty hall on the ground floor. Up in the tower, a tiny rectangle at floor level permits sunbeams to play around your feet. To get to the lavatory you sometimes have to push open a dozen vast and powerfully sprung doors. The lift sometimes stops at forgotten levels where dust and dust sheets shroud ancient filing cabinets and one can imagine shrivelled academics decomposing behind locked doors.

It was in an improbable and gloomy chamber on the ground floor that I first met my tutor Michael Cohen. Bright staff smiles flashed democratic mateyness. The groups to be attached to each tutor were read out, and rallying points indicated about the room. I joined my group.

'Sit down, sit down,' says the tutor. And, 'my name is Cohen', deep drag on a tiny cigarette. 'Yes, please smoke if you do.'

A scuffle of matches and the gloom of the room becomes deeper and bluer. Mr Cohen adjusts a pad of paper on his knee.

'Now,' he looks around the group with a smile of almost toxic friendliness, 'I want you to give me your names, and ...' the smile-intensity is somehow incredibly increased, '... and not just your surname, but your christian name or the name by which you prefer to be called.'

'Oh God,' I think, 'one of them.'

And other thoughts come to mind.

My name has always been difficult to pronounce, for me. And I am tempted to suggest that I really like to be called Spud or Spike. It would make a good story afterwards. But I feel panic rising as my turn approaches. Sure enough, as always happens I pitch my voice too soft. When asked to repeat, I produce a series of spittle-less consonants.

'Nchlstt.'

At the third attempt in desperation I shout my name, making the students in the next group jump in the smokey darkness.

Thank God that's over.

I am affronted by that assumption of a relationship which doesn't exist. Naming is a symptom – a symbol – of the reality beneath. You can't alter the relationship by messing around with the symbols. If I called him 'darling', would he grow to love me?

There is a whirling storm of jargon every Friday morning. It seems as though the whole of the student-teacher world converges on the Institute for this barrage of lectures. There are far too many people for the decayed cinema of a lecture hall, so they are dispersed about the building in dimly-lit caverns and the lectures are relayed by loudspeaker systems. I have never felt so disconnected from the source of the educational spring! We sit in rows facing nothing. People do crosswords, drink coffee and chat because that mechanical bellowing can drown and ignore everything.

Then we get interference in the wires or some fault suddenly reduces the lecturer's voice to a faint insect scratching in the dim distance. We conscientious students come to life on these occasions and nudge each other and laugh like happy half-wits.

And when you can hear it, the jargon is amazing, stunning. Sociology comes top, of course.

'The internalization of the achievement ethic, and the democratization of the means of education . . .' and all that.

And there is much flatulent rational philosophy about 'normative criteria' and 'initiation into intrinsically worthwhile activities', and 'cognitive perspectives'.

But in English teaching the word is 'creative'. Creativity, creative writing, creative thinking, creative drama, etc., etc. I have been unable to work out exactly what they might mean by this, but so far it seems to designate 'good' writing done by schoolchildren. The opposite of compositions of the dreary 'O' level kind. It seems to be, therefore, a value-judgement word.

And Mr Cohen has suggested that the tutor group do some of it!

'It seems odd,' he said, 'that an art master should be expected to be able to paint, while no one ever even asks if an English teacher writes anything other than letters of application and reports.'

This is so devastatingly obvious that I feel impelled to pretend that I have thought of it before. The fact that I have not thought of it also means that I am very suspicious of it.

'So,' he goes on, 'how about it? I want you to do some writing during the course, and we will read it in the group, and talk about it, and about what it was like writing it and so on. So that we will have some experience of what the task we ask children to undertake, is really like.'

If the pumping of my heart is anything to go by, there is panic abroad in the group. There is a tense silence which I know will break at coffee time.

'For the first piece of writing I am going to set a theme, and it is an educational one. I would like you to write, in any way you wish, about an experience from your education which was memorable, or from which you think you learned something. Okay?'

We troop off for coffee muttering outraged complaints, 'What does he think we are?' ... 'It's just typical of this bloody establishment' ... 'Do they honestly think all good teachers are poets or something?' ... And I think 'Right mate – I'll show you – I'll put you, Mr Cohen, on paper, so straight and so cruel and yet so subtly disguised, that though we will all know who is talking about whom, you won't even be able to acknowledge the fact. We'll see about democratic staff–student stuff ... see whether you really mean it.'

And what is more I actually did it. I pretended I was writing about my school days and about a new American physics master who greeted the kids with a 'smile of almost toxic friendliness' and demanded to know their 'christian names or the names by which they preferred to be called'.

When the time comes for the pieces to be read everyone is tense. A high proportion of the pieces are simply about the process of writing the actual pieces of writing (interesting that) and as my turn approaches my heart is pounding at my own audacity. Surely, I think, my little story is bound to be recognized for its insolence.

But whether Mr Cohen sees it that way is not at all apparent. He makes some shrewd answers to criticisms by other members of the group who say that it is not what was asked for. And none of the others rush up afterwards and say 'How did you dare?' or 'You *are* a one!' Gradually I surprise myself becoming aware of having really enjoyed writing and reading it. And I also reflect that one's own view of events is a very personal thing. People don't see themselves as others do.

(Some time after the event I came round to wondering how Mr Cohen would have written about our group of budding English teachers, and about the callow long-nosed one who was so prickly and hostile.)

Creativity grinds on at us. What I don't like about it all is the inspiration notion. They, the Institute specialists, seem to think that creative writing is something that arises spontaneously from the experience of the writer. The teacher ploughs up the compost of the memories of the pupils, at the crucial moment he says 'Write', and up sprouts all this poetry and intensely-felt personal stuff. The place of objectivity is in discursive as opposed to creative writing.

I can't help thinking that this is all missing some essential point. In my painting, which I regard as creative, I have just made some advance by rigorous thought, experiment, rejection and revision. I think I could have waited for ever for deeper understanding and insight to blossom spontaneously. I had to take a grip, argue with friends about what a picture was and what it could be, and most important of all for *my* painting, I had to analyse the conventions of formal representation on a flat surface and think hard about the interaction of colour in respect of hue, tone, intensity and so on.

Similarly with music, it was not until I was forced to analyse how arm movements, pressure, bow speed, vibrato and so on, altered the noises that a violin can make, that I began to be able to make noises which were appropriate to the musical context.

Well, I'm proud of this thinking, and of what it has produced in terms of 'creativity'. And the fact that my pictures are now sometimes exhibited and bought seems a seal of recognition that the thinking behind them is not rubbish. So the apparently facile use of the word 'creative' puts me off. I wish they would examine *their* basic assumptions rather more publicly.

The discussion in the group is almost never successful. Mr Cohen says something challenging, or reads us something and then says 'Well, what do you think about that?'

The silence is solid. If the experience of the others is like mine, we sit there while the silence builds up a psychic pressure inside our skulls until someone, usually me at the moment, makes some world-shattering comment which seems either obvious or irrelevant or both. Mr Cohen fishes out another of his tiny fags, says 'Hmph' and the silence continues. I wonder whether the others are thinking about the subject or are wondering whether the rest of us are thinking about it. I recall attempts at group seminars on poetry at Cambridge, which were abandoned at the second attempt by my supervisor. 'Is it me?' I wonder. Can Socratic dialogue ever have actually occurred?

Someone says something and Mr Cohen seizes on it gratefully and, Socratic dialogue forgotten, we have a Platonic monologue instead. It is interesting, but *why* no discussion? I know I am afraid of being obvious, of saying things which surely everyone else must have thought. It is difficult to know where to begin to discuss a topic like 'What does language do for you when you use it for personal writing?'

I want to start in at the point of some new uncommunicated ideas of mine about how language imposes order on your experience. But the thing I want to say is that the order imposed by the language which you have inherited for describing experience may not be the order of the universe. And that the fact that language has order and coherence need not mean that your experience had. Or does it?

Eventually, temples pounding, I stammer out the first bit, which immediately becomes the text for a bit of a lecture from Mr Cohen. I sit boiling while *my* idea is elaborated, and when with an ill-judged glance in my direction he concludes with

'Do you understand?'

I say 'Yes' with a shrug of such resentment that he takes the point.

And next time? Square one, and all that pressure in the skull again.

There is another thing connected with creativity. The word seems to go so closely with improvisation and folkery. There is improvised drama and mention of improvised music 'as in folk-art'. I suffered at Cambridge with a don who had given up the study of the entrails of crustacea in favour of the scratchings of Black Sea fiddlers and I am a little hysterical on the subject of folk music. He regarded improvisation as the essential thing about expression in art. As though the folk music were greater than Bach. Indeed he claimed he would rather have the gipsy fiddlers themselves than the sophistication of the gipsy idiom in the Haydn or Bartok string quartets.

'Improvised' sounds faintly pejorative to me. Not so to the Institute!

Also surely it is more often a recombination of remembered elements, than an original new thing, as its apparent spontaneity would seem to suggest.

We have to write a long essay on our special subject over Christmas. I'm going to do a grand tour of Logic, Ethics and Aesthetics, and prove to my special-subject tutor that they are really all one thing. What pretension! But I don't want to do one of those piddling essays which shows you have understood someone else's ideas. Not this time anyway.

With a tightening of the stomach I realize that teaching practice begins very soon now. We have scarcely met any real live children. In fact only one or two short visits to a comprehensive school in the East End. My chief memory of these is of the group trooping into the school building to the cockney jeers of some second formers. One counted us off with extravagant gestures.

'Stu – dent, stu – dent, stu – dent', and with that falling mocking cadence children use to taunt.

I have to keep a diary during my teaching practice. Mr Cohen said (one could have predicted it):

'I don't mean the kind of thing you may have heard about where you set out each lesson under headings – Aim – Method – Achievement. Rather something which simply contains your impressions, pieces of writing about what you did and what happened to you. Anything which interested you or surprised you; and the way in which you do it is up to you.'

He then gave us some duplicated extracts from a diary kept by a previous student.

In spite of my audacity over the creative writing, I think I will keep my official diary in another book.

Extract from teaching diary

Monday

First day. Everyone has been most helpful. Mr Fenton almost unbelievably so. Students seem (so far) to be positively welcome at Hershamfleet Grammar School. The school is in pleasant bungaloid modern buildings which spider over a gently sloping site. After the improvised homely muddle of the public school I went to, this place seems very thoroughly planned and equipped. The area, I gather, is average 'nice' suburban. I *think* I know what that means.

The forms I am to teach show a good if rather top-heavy spread.

Two periods per week with 1Z (the Z is ominous in a school that uses streaming, but in fact it indicates that the lower forms 1, 2 and 3 are unstreamed). One of these is what is called 'mime' in the hall.

Two classes with 3X with whom I am to use the course book.

Two classes with T4. 'T' stands for 'Technical' and means by some fascinating semantic shift, 'bottom stream'. Mrs Blake, with whom I saw them this morning, has rather despaired of them, I think. Actually they appeared to react fairly well when she read Wilfred Owen to them, and they seemed to have a fair amount of knockabout humour in them. There is one girl who is a compulsive writer – and not a bad one.

'Why did you write sixteen pages, Pat?'

' 'Cos I like writing.'

Suppressed moans from the rest of the class. It is perhaps indicative of something that they have been saddled with *Mr Polly*, for which, I gather, they show a healthy contempt. Since I have to teach it them, I shall have to devise some anti-Polly lessons or see if I can't shelve it.

Three lessons each with Lower 6A and Lower 6B. I am to plan courses of lessons to cover the four weeks I shall be at the school this term. I thought a course on the sonnet and a course on something else to last half the number of periods and to be exchanged between the classes at half-time. This requires work, but once again 'they' have been more than cooperative; Mr Felton sprinted off for a wax sheet for the duplicator, etc.

Finally, one lesson a week with an upper-sixth general English class. This contains linguists, scientists and some A-level English pupils. This morning I observed a lesson where they were reading *Which?*–type reports on soap, matches and Saturday newspapers. Competent stuff, but apart from some flashes of wit sending up the whole exercise, in the report on matches, it was rather dim – in fact damned dull. (That's a first impression.) I thought I might see what they made of types of language. It might clear my own mind on the subject.

Tuesday

I taught two classes today; neither was a success. When I said I had been asked to do *The History of Mr Polly* with them, T4 broke into a heartrending group moan. I can remember that moan from my own schooldays. 'Come on,' the teacher would say, 'get out your English books.' And magically the whole class would produce a low defeated sound – 'Gnawww.' I had no idea how demoralizing it was for the teacher. I started by being unfair about Wells. We looked at the introduction where there were some interesting remarks about his reaction to the First World War. He was a member of Lord Northcliffe's Enemy Propaganda Committee. One of the boys defined propaganda as 'lies'. There was a flicker of interest over 'lies about the Enemy Committee'. But a reference on my part to the Owen poems they had been reading yesterday killed the flicker. I wonder why?

3X, friendly but unruly. I've never tried such a large class before – twenty-nine is not considered large in the state system! – I tried a slightly fatuous exercise from the course book. They certainly had the measure of it; or rather those who did seemed to resent being asked such obvious questions, and those who did not, left it to those who did, to do the answering.

I shall not get my sixth-form material ready by the time I meet them on Thursday. My one-fingered typing can't cope. It will have to be what the Institute calls an 'orientation period'.

Wednesday
Five hours' mud and rain to Liverpool. Five hours' mud, rain and fog back again.

That last entry conceals the unpedagogical excitement of seeing one of my pictures on the wall of a large gallery beside other works by people with Famous Names. I get a deep thrill from such silly things as seeing my name in print in the catalogue, or receiving a little slip saying:

Many directors of galleries will be invited to the exhibition; and we shall encourage them to buy from it. It would be helpful if you would indicate on the enclosed post card whether you would agree to a reduction of 10 per cent in the purchase price of your work if it is sold to a public gallery or other public body such as the Arts Council.

Fridays are still fraught with the jargon barrages in the morning. In the afternoon we collect again with Mr Cohen and have a discussion session about how the teaching has gone.

I feel now that I am more cagey than the rest of the group. Where we were discussing abstracts I was afraid to speak but I had something to say, and I saw no point in dishonesty if I was going to say anything. But in discussing what we have actually been doing there are all kinds of other pressures to encourage mendacity. I just shrug and say 'Well, it didn't go as well as I'd have liked.' Trying to sound like an air ace referring to a 'bit of a nonsense actually'.

Annette, at the other extreme talks with alarming candour and total disregard for the liberal, child-centred ethos of the Institute.

'Well, I don't know but they seem to me to be a bunch of ill-mannered noisy brats. They *would* not shut up and listen. What? ... Well they *ought* to have been interested. When I was at school, I would never even have considered talking to the teacher like that even if it was only a student. No. I certainly wouldn't. I wouldn't have dared.'

Extract from teaching diary

Thursday

Three sixth-form classes today. Even with these small groups it is difficult to get a discussion going. However, there were signs of life by the end of the Technical fourth lesson. I asked them what sort of essay they would choose to write – what *they* would *really* like to write about. Typical answers were 'Character sketch' followed by three more identical answers from kids who didn't know what the question was. Then 'horror story' or 'thriller' offered to see what the reaction would be, or to get a laugh from the rest of the class. Then 'description of a place'. When I asked him why he wanted to do that, 'Because it's easy. You've got to do a homework; it might as well take as little time as possible.'

It was only after the class was over that they came rushing up individually, and said breathless and confidential, 'can I do ...' or 'could we do ...'

So perhaps there is hope.

Monday

L6A: We started on the Sonnet course. They were more than unwilling to commit themselves. Indeed they would only offer a reply to a question if they could include words like 'imagery' or 'personification'. Of course they can have little experience which would help them share this sophisticated attitude towards love. How, after all, can they be wittily objective about it?

Do they above love to be loved and yet
Those lovers scorn whom that love doth possess?

Interestingly they preferred Christina Rossetti. They did not even suffer semantic saturation over:

Aloof, aloof, we stand aloof, so stand
Thou too aloof . . .

I thought of loofahs and improbable situations.

The lower-stream group L6B are amusing and voluble. Quite different. Jennifer says it is silly to write songs about love and then admits a fashionable addiction to pop. She is understandably irritated by any attempt to conclude an inconsistency from these facts. After all the pop song has a social function.

Tuesday

T4 started to write. Some of them were alarmingly intent. I have been warned not to expect a direct correlation between intensity of application and quality of end product. Noise only reached a certain ceiling contributed to by about half the class. Some regarded the lesson as a soft option. Two sat with dim, clouded faces doing nothing.

'Clearly cases for individual attention' think I, brightly.

What did they do with their weekends? 'Don't know', they reply in tones heavy with guilt.

'What would they rather be doing than an English lesson?' 'Don't know' they reply, arms folded, looking dully at the grimy floor and then at the ceiling

'Why,' I wonder. 'What do these answers mean? Are they social cyphers with a meaning such as 'do not disturb'?

3X I read an extract from *Bandoola* and Ted Hughes's *Pike*. Told them to write. One small knot of girls became progressively more hysterical. But, in general, an amazingly large proportion seemed to do some work.

When they ask 'Can I do something about an owl?', they
are clearly not asking permission – they are seeing,
perhaps, how the idea sounds as a public utterance.
Compare 'Can I give it a surprise ending?'

They wrote today telling me they had sold my picture. What an
odd sensation it is. Someone went to see the exhibition and decided to buy my painting. Someone who knows no more about
me than my name and my picture. I wonder if he is tall or thin or
short or fat or red or sallow. I wonder did he think it was an
investment and have I got responsibilities towards him. Or was it
the first picture he had ever bought and did he just do it and
surprise himself?

Extract from teaching diary

Wednesday

L6A were very dozy. Those who had made some
comments before were totally silent today. Worst of all was
the tall boy Benskin. Red-rimmed eyes; set mouth; grey
skin; silent fixed stare at a point at infinity. Immovable. An
anger of despair started in my solar plexus.

3X listened to the tape recording of *Lord of the Flies*
quite well. And for the space of five minutes at the end of
the lesson, they discussed it quite well, too. By the time the
bell went there was some deterioration in quality – but
there is a subtle change in their behaviour from the last
lesson. The results of their predatory animals essays were
not bad. Some good expression:
The hawk 'a bundle of instant death'.
A kingfisher looking into a lake, 'found a flashing slither
glinting in the light'.
But on the other hand, what does one make of this: 'Not
for food did the cat kill, but because rats were germ
carriers'?

Among others which were not remarkable for linguistic
control there was a great deal of enthusiasm for working
out the full implications of a situation. For example, what

happens when a party of natives fall out of their canoe, if the river is occupied by an incredibly well organized posse of crocodiles?

4th Extra: This was a stand-in lesson for someone else who was away. I arrived full of enthusiasm and confidence and with the feeling that I was going to give them a great treat. I was going to give them stacks of material and ask them to choose what they liked with a view to reading it and discussing it. I was going to. . . . But I discovered that they'd been doing exactly that, with that very material, and were 'fed up' with it. Fortunately they were expecting a reading lesson and had brought their own books. So they read . . . while I deflated.

T4: This was to have been watched by Mr Cohen, so more than usual care had gone into its preparation. First we read a magnificently gory piece of Hazlitt about a prize fight between Neate and the Gasman. The discussion started slowly, but the quotation, 'This is the high and heroic state of man,' split the class down the middle; boys in favour, girls against. From there we went to Cassius Clay, the Wild Man of Borneo, the audiences of wrestling, etc. At times it even resembled discussion, though disagreement was normally voiced as 'you don't know what you're talking about, so shut up!'

Monday

Roger on Teachers   T4

Teachers are like the weather, one minute good, one minute bad. Some teachers are always good, some are always bad. Quite a lot of teachers are not very nice and give out essays and detentions for the slightest reasons, and do it with a big grin across their faces. Other teachers are alright, they can take a joke and still keep the class under control. A few others just can't handle children and the children play about and no work is done. Some teachers stick strictly to the rules and if anybody puts a foot out of line, they are pounced on and dealt with.

Few teachers treat you as your age, but as little children. Some teachers you can have a good talk to, others not.

You are the pupil, they are the teacher, they are the best, we aren't.

It is like this all through your school career until you leave and then they say these were the best days of your life.

Tuesday

T4 were much better. I read Roger's piece to them and they were considerably impressed. We had quite an orderly discussion, and when I mentioned writing the moan was clearly a formality. Even the ones who last week 'did not know' about anything, were writing quite hard.

3X: This was a curious lesson. I read them *First Flight* by Vernon Scannell, I revived their memories of the piece about the prize fight, and we tried a discussion. Fairly chaotic – less good than T4 in fact. So I set them to writing. It was then that the curious part occurred. There was the usual initial hubbub which seemed to be gradually quietening down as I wandered around talking to the uncertain ones. Then, when I was talking to some of the girls, one of the boys pinched someone's geometry set.

'Ooze got my geometry set?'

'Give it 'ere!'

'I ain't got it!'

And so on . . . a crescendo which outraged the schoolmaster in me. The first thing I did was to steer the attention away from the geometry set, by pointing out that it was not necessary for an English essay and that he could retrieve it after the lesson anyway.

No effect – more, increased noise.

I got the attention of them all and gave a schoolmasterly little speech feeling idiotic and pompous, and recalling all the time my own reactions to similar incidents in my schooldays.

No effect. As soon as I finished the noise continued unabated. So I thought, 'What next?' Clearly a repetition of the speech would not serve. My nerves were on stalks; I kept glancing at the glass panel in the door to see if my shame was being overheard.

Then, without my doing anything at all, the noise quite suddenly subsided. Everyone in the room was writing. If they conversed now it was about the work and *in whispers*.

Why?

The geometry set, which was clearly only a pretext, was now forgotten. I almost got the feeling that the class acted according to its own inaccessible group laws. It was like watching a shoal of fish which in their other element suddenly take a group decision, and swim off for no reason you can grasp. There had been no leadership by one boy; no response to an outside influence; they had totally ignored me.

At University I felt lost when I had to do an essay. I always put it off to the very last minute and I can remember actually beating my head against the cold wall of my lodgings when I could find nothing to say about Dryden. I had read my Dryden, always hoping for something which I did not find, and I had groped through an impenetrable book about his intellectual milieu – and I had nothing to say. In a less extreme form this was my weekly experience and in shame and desperation I squeezed some cliches like toothpaste from an exhausted tube, onto the page. In the subsequent tutorial I was defensive about my efforts, without conviction. I can only remember one exception to this general rule and that was, ironically, an essay on the seventeenth-century sermon. Here I had found something to say and I had not found it said anywhere else and I read my essay with triumphant conviction to my tutor, a man distinguished internationally for his work on communications.

'You enjoyed writing that, did you?' he asked. I nodded in breathless anticipation of the heady intellectual discussion that must surely follow. 'Well,' he went on dismissively, 'how about a glass of sherry?'

And that was that.

I feel a bit that way about my special subject essay. I want it to be good, and I want it to be appreciated!

I read Roger's piece on teachers to our group of students, at our Friday afternoon session with Mr Cohen. They said he'd got his subject weighed up, and someone commented on the logical anti-

thesis in the style. One person noticed what must be the unconscious irony of the teaching jargon:

'If anyone puts a foot out of line they are pounced on and
dealt with' . . .

I can hear the tone there, and see the pedagogical frown and
gesture.

What stays with me is the sad shrug in the end:

'It is like this all through your school career until you leave,
and then they say these were the best days of your life.'

What is also ironic is that the reading of the piece seemed to
gain me some kind of prestige in the group . . . as though I was
being successful. In fact my chief emotion as I drive to Hershamfleet every morning is one of gratitude that the four-week
practice session is so short and so nearly over.

Extract from teaching diary

iZ: I had a go at this creative drama business in the hall. I
wonder what the hell it is all about. I asked somebody for a
suggestion or two beforehand, and they offered the idea of
well known stories to be acted out.

So, 'get into groups' I bawled. 'Make a short play out of
the Good Samaritan, or Little Red Riding Hood, or David
and Goliath or the crossing of the Red Sea, or . . .'

For the rest of the lesson I might as well have not been
there. One group did a splendid Good Samaritan, though
the fight was by far the best and longest bit. The crossing-
of-the-Red-Sea group turned the hall chairs into chariots
for the occasion, and held chariot races from the
Samaritan to Goliath and back again. A third group spent
the entire lesson gloomily debating the relative dramatic
merits of Goldilocks and Little Red Riding Hood (their
interest in it amazed me). The fourth group in a dim
corner acted David and Goliath over and over again. With
a kind of dreamy languor, David socked Goliath on the
jaw and he collapsed fairly impressively for a moment.
Immediately they swopped parts and acted the same brief
tale. Four podgy female Philistines leaned their bottoms

against a radiator and looked on in mild contentment. One
sheepish Israelite acted the part of a referee who has
forgotten the rules. The whole thing looked like an
endlessly repeated loop film of a pub-brawl.

What were they learning?

L6 1: In these lessons I suffer the other end of the Michael
Cohen discussion agony. I ask question after question and
they all breed silence and fixed stares.

Mr Felton said: 'When you ask a question such as:
"What do you think, Pauline?", and the response is dead
silence, it is often because you have not made the area of
thought sufficiently clear. Or you have not directed the
pupils' thinking to a sufficiently small area for them to see
the kind of comment you want.' That seems true. Doubt
breeds silence. Most of them will answer a question like:
'What day is it?' with confident relief.

But surely silence is not the best response to doubt and
uncertainty in an educational situation? Why can't they
say: 'What are you on about?' or 'I can't see what you are
driving at.'

But then why can't we teachers do it in Mr Cohen's
tutorial groups? What is this pressure to be silent?

And in any case all these questions I ask myself in this
diary breed a deep puzzled silence in my own mind.

What is this pressure to be silent?

Well, words like 'shyness', 'diffidence' describe the cause
in some cases. But a description is a rephrasing of 'pressure
to be silent'. Where does that get us? Another question.

It all seems to open up still more questions about our
psychology, the philosophy of the curriculum.

We have been asked to hand in our diaries.

Well, we must do it I suppose.

I have looked through my teaching diary and tried to sort out
what I think about it. It is dishonest, of course – otherwise I
would not be keeping a parallel expanded version of it. On the
other hand it is more honest than I would have thought probable
two months ago. I have been in the pupil-student situation too
long to imagine that total honesty gets you very far. But at least it

has not been falsified by an AIM – METHOD – CONTENT type of formula. That breeds mendacity if you like.

e.g. You drive to school with a hangover and find yourself totally unprepared in front of thirty screaming second formers. You ask them how they react to strangers and at the end of the lesson you collapse gratefully in the common room until break-time, while your nerves pop and snap and your stomach contracts and twitches at the memory of the chaos your question seemed to set loose. Then you fish out your diary in the evening.

AIM: To enlarge the children's awareness of the stressful nature of encounters with unknown individuals. To expand this towards an understanding of the relation between socio-economic and/or ethnic differentials, and the degree of stress experienced.

METHOD: A loose discussion format was adopted, with the children alternating between group involvement, individual initiative and total class participation.

CONTENT: The discussion relied mainly on the individual experiences of the children with the occasional anecdote supplied by the teacher to lead onto new ground.

COMMENTS: To be critical of the lesson, it was rather episodic and the language evoked tended to be narrative or expletive. Descriptive material was reserved for passages of abuse.

Now, why is that a spoof? It *is* a spoof, though I have read passages like it in progressive journals about English teaching. I have a hunch it would not go down well with Michael Cohen – even if I strung it all together and left out the headings.

Without the AIM – METHOD – CONTENT format how does one write the ideal diary entry? For Mr Cohen it should perhaps be a poem?

Chalk-dust fought with the cobwebs
In my mind this morning.
No morning's minion, I
Fought 2C, and
Fought to see the *why*.
'Strangers,' I cried . . .

And the aptness jogged
My grey lethargy to panic.
'Aw, sir . . .' ' 'e kicked me . . .'
'My dad's got the sack . . .'
This won't do . . . there's that window
At my back.
'Strangers, well, tramps
And negroes, foreigners, the
Rich! . . . for God's sake
Shut your flaming little traps.'
And after break, when I must fight
2B
Must I fight again
To be?

How about *that* for a 'with-it' diary entry? But I would never actually *do* it. I can only be daring where it does not really touch me and discipline is a bogey still. Is it always like this?

That ideal diary entry. Mendacious certainly, but mendacious within the context of the Institute's ethos. Let me see.

'This second-year group I have on Tuesdays' . . . right informal, intimate tone . . . 'seems to me to have leadership trouble' . . . puzzled humility . . . 'I really must look into the sociometry angle . . . read Moreno and see whether groupings arrived at that way don't improve matters' . . . reference to other lectures in an experimental spirit . . . 'I must admit I was not at my best when I tackled the strangers project with them' . . . more humility and self awareness there, but a subtle hint that 'strangers' was not just the first word to come to mind through that hangover fog. '. . . but none the less, there was too much irrelevance, too much abuse and too little rigorous thought.'

I think that might do. And the appalling thing is that it is in exactly that tone that my official teaching diary is written. I thought I was being more honest than that!

So what would an ideal entry be? I always think of what I think *they* would want. And in the school it is different from in the Institute. Do the pupils try to think of what *I* want when I ask them to write? Perhaps an ideal answer *should* be a poem after all, only a real one – a great piece of writing. Perhaps all writers have to face this opposition of what is true and what they think the reader – even an ideal reader – will want to read. And yet in my situation, as I am, now, at the Institute, it would hardly serve my limited ends with regard to the certificate I hope to attain, to be honest. And if my ideas were more at variance with those popular at the Institute it would be even less in my interest.

For the record (for this private record) the poem, for all its frivolity, is the truest account of the three.

Spring term

I spent the vacation on my long essay on philosophy. It really is a magnificently heady piece of pretentiousness. I've never taken any piece of work so seriously and I've never done so much work. I bought a special folder and special foolscap paper. Doing this is a kind of luxury I really enjoy. Buying stationery seems like a pledge of a serious intention in life – it makes me feel important. I can cheer myself up for five or ten shillings any day, just by purchasing a notebook and a file.

I chatted with my furry philosophy tutor to get a reading list. A lady colleague of his came into the room while I was there and he introduced me by saying, 'This is Mr Otty. He is going to sort out aesthetics for us, Ho! Ho!' while my flesh crept.

Anyway, look how organized I was. The whole opus is called Logic, Ethics and Aesthetics. It is divided into sections,

1. Introduction (which concludes magnificently 'So the argument is personal – it focuses on "I" – it can make no real appeal to an external logical framework; but in order to give it a flavour of philosophy I will attempt to generalize this fact, and show why it is necessarily the nature of moral and aesthetic judgements.'!)
2. The rational ethic.
3. The rational aesthetic.
4. Pernicious effects of failing to distinguish between ethics and aesthetics. (Which is a finely ironical demolition of J. Stolnitz who appeared on my furry friend's reading list.)
5. Logics, ethics and aesthetics.
6. A breathing space introducing my own ideas.
7. Where Art and Morality meet (!!!)

The whole occupies twelve and a half sides of foolscap and has footnotes and references galore.

So I hand it in and wait with bated breath for 'furry' to read it and comment. When I do get it back it has the following written on it:

B? + An interesting and original account, which runs up against some fundamental issues in philosophy. Your argument unfortunately becomes rather obscure towards the end.

I feel that for a question of this magnitude you need to acquire some of the techniques you could get from a more rigorous training in philosophy.

Are you interested in the Academic Diploma?

The text was decorated in the margin with remarks like: 'I find this rather obscure,' and 'It is not clear what your position is.' And little vertical bars and question-marks.

I try to analyse why I am so cross and disappointed. I struggle with contradictory descriptions of him as 'Brilliant – well of course he must be, or he would not be in his present post,' and on the other hand, 'He's a twit. He grew his beard to hide his personality problems. And he could not abandon his rigid rationalism for long enough to encompass my vision, because it is only that rationalism which permits him to carry on,' and 'He has decided that there are certain fallacies detectable in philosophical discourse, and his main source of pleasure is detecting those fallacies in the work of great men.'

I think the most deadly thing about his reaction is his evident lack of real interest in what I have to say. If he meant the words 'interesting and original' surely he would talk about it with me. Surely he would not just put B?+. And what the hell does ? mean?

But then perhaps he was just being kind. He *must* have been. Because if a philosopher really encounters something interesting and original, surely he pursues it? He must have meant: (let's rephrase it . . .)

B (grudgingly + (for neatness?)). A dull and hackneyed piece of work. But I suppose that any uninitiated person who actually *encounters* some of the basic issues in philosophy must be trying quite hard.

Clearly you don't know much about how to think, but if you join my course for the Academic Diploma, I can help you to become one of us.

No. That is callow and unworthy. And I can see that he prob-ably does know what is wrong with my essay. It is just that I have committed so much to it that I cannot accept his dismissal with a good grace.

More creativity. This time Michael Cohen has suggested we make a tape. We take a theme and put together a series of items of poetry, music, improvised dialogue, which in the end says some-thing about the theme. All the other tutor groups are doing the same kind of thing and we are to have a session when we play them all and, no doubt, discuss them.

Since the idea started, most of the group have shown a pretty spectacular lack of interest. Some have said they'll take care of the poetry and some have thought of some music but there was no opposition to Janet's initial suggestion that we should group it all round the theme of 'Strangers'.

Janet is interesting. She is the oldest member of the group and while declaring as hearty a contempt as the rest of us for all that we are required by the Institute to perform, she nevertheless ac-tually *does* far more and in a far more whole-hearted kind of way.

Anyway it looks as though she and I are to do the dialogue part of it all. I have been a middle-European gentleman looking for Tottenham Court Road, and getting a variety of unhelpful answers from Janet in different disguised voices. Then she is being a Geordie market researcher asking fatuous questions about some product while I, in a number of assumed voices, declare my patrician disdain, or my unhelpful and misdirected plebeian interest. On the tape our interviews are to be punctuated with suitable chunks of the Beatles (*He's a real nowhere man . . .*) and Dylan. For poetry, things like Tessimond on the British.

It's an idea, certainly, and if it were really master-minded by some master mind it could produce really good results, I think. It might well be worth a try in school.

Now the idea is stories. Well, I am less shocked than I was when Michael first asked me to write, and Janet and I took him to lunch in the Lamb and chatted him up a bit which made things more human, so this time I feel I'll have a go.

Janet says she is being 'social realist' about a demolition-gang labourer with symbolic overtones – and from what the others say I think very few of them will write at all. I don't want to do nothing; but I don't want to be the good boy doing all my homework to please teacher. So I shall attack the idea of stories. I'll make it sufficiently strange and silly for the group to be uncertain how to take it – and that will provide a defence for me to hide behind as well. No one will dare to sneer in case they are caught on the wrong foot.

I have an idea about the way the world falls apart when I've arranged to meet someone and they fail to turn up. I don't mean an important meeting – I mean just *any* meeting. There you are standing around, wondering what's gone wrong until you begin to wonder how you know what day it is, or who you are and so on.

'Hum . . . about my brain.'

We put the tape together this afternoon in one of the Institute's cellars. It took hours, but through all the giggles and false starts and feedback beeping noises, the procedure did generate a kind of 'esprit' in the group.

In the end, in spite of all our defensivenesses, our sneers and protective irony, we were quite pleased with ourselves.

I also detected in myself a kind of competitive hope that it would be the best tape when we play them all . . . I find that fact both nauseating and exciting at the same time!

We read our stories today. Here is mine. In spite of my avowed intention to needle the group, I enjoyed writing this, and I think it says a lot of what I think. It is called:

Not at Home

They would meet at James's flat at 5.45 and go on from there to the pub. Philip made an entry in his diary for the following Wednesday:

'James, 5.45', it said.

'Fine,' he said, 'see you then.'

Between 11.43 p.m. on Monday, when the dramatic incident outlined above took place, and 5.45 p.m. on the following Wednesday, Time, in spite of masculine gender and extreme old age, gave birth to many and varied events. Watching clock or watch would have made it possible to notice the passage of forty-two hours and two minutes.

Now Philip is our central concern here, and he averaged three blinks of each eye per minute during his waking hours and seventy-eight to eighty-six more or less beats of his heart whether awake or asleep; and so we can see that if this is to remain a short story, and although we are concerned with Philip, there is much of vital concern to Philip which cannot deeply concern us. We must select.

There was the continuous intimate energy exchange of his autonomous self; the scarlet secrets of the haemoglobin; the churning and bubbling of the gastric juices achieving the occasional dignity of eructation; the long slow ripple of the peristalsis. And there were events of more immediate concern. The inconceivable rapidity with which nerve jarred nerve and nerve galvanized muscle into spasm and from spasm into soggy relaxation as he stumbled up the stairs of the bus on the Monday night; the pressure on his hamstrings, which was pleasant until it gave him pins and needles, as he sat extended after lunch on the Tuesday. And there were series of events which Philip's mind unconsciously amalgamated into states of affairs. A series of signals of pain received when the tip of his tongue made contact with hot tea or coffee, became amalgamated into the concept of a state of roughness which the tip was suffering. And he boldly proposed to himself a causal relationship between that state and a series of explorations of a cavity in an upper molar. And this implied an acceptance which he did not make conscious of a state of affairs in the cosmos, which permitted causation.

So we have selected some events to be noted as a ground from which the figure of our hero will emerge. To put it another way, these are bits of the evidence which helped Philip to imagine processes, the imagining of which led him to believe, as he walked down the street on Wednesday at 5.44 p.m., that he was the same person as had walked up the same street at 11.44 p.m. on the Monday.

As he approached the door of the house in which James's flat was situated and as he prepared to press the bell-push with James's name beside it, Philip might have said to himself,

'The world is like a loom.'

or

'My days are swifter than a weaver's shuttle.'

But he did not. Because, one might say, his mental picture of reality was not sufficiently different from his mental picture of a loom, Philip pressed the bell by James's blue front door, and waited, empty of the illumination of metaphor.

On pressing a door bell you may listen for its ringing. But if it rings in the top floor flat of a densely populated and complexly compartmented Victorian house, you will hear nothing. You may wait for banging doors, approaching footsteps, shouts, screams. But if only three steps and a pavement segregate you from grinding buses and honking taxis, you will hear nothing. So Philip imagined the bell, the stairs, the doors, and plotted James's movements. He recalled, and vividly saw as if projected on the back of his eyeballs how James raised his left eyebrow at the sound of the bell; how he rarely answered it directly but was wont to do some household chore on the way: how he would empty the wastepaper basket or fill a cigarette lighter, or pour Harpic into the lavatory bowl, or stale beer out of the window, as though these actions needed for their accomplishment an external impetus to overcome inertia. He would then go to the door of the flat, which opened directly on to the attic stair. He would try each of the doorknobs in turn before remembering that it was necessary to turn a certain combination of knobs in order to open the door. So he would wedge whatever he had been pouring from or emptying or filling under his arm or between his knees and he would try the top knob simultaneously with the middle knob. Then he would try the top knob with the bottom knob. Then the middle knob with the bottom knob. Because the door opened outwards he would then pirouette rapidly and gracelessly through 180 degrees and land on the fourth step down. Beer jug, waste-paper basket or cigarette lighter was usually retained during this operation, imposing a further inelegance on his final posture. Mrs Druggett, summoned by the crash through velvet curtains would demand, with fat and ugly threats, her rent.

If this much detail is tedious to the reader he must remember Philip's need. He must bear with Philip while his mind conjures still more detail of James, having subdued Mrs Druggett, stopping just beyond the door in the subaqueous gloom of the hall, to blow his nose thoroughly and at length and to examine, in detail, the results, and how although it seemed James could only proceed from this action to the opening of the front door, yet Philip could see him, on a chance impulse, picking up and thumbing through a heap of dusty and ancient football coupons, bills, tax forms and licence reminders. The reader must bear with Philip, because even after all this imagining and all the time it took, the blue front door remained closed.

The blue front door remained closed, so James was not at home. Or James was ill; or James was dead. Or Philip was at the wrong house: at the wrong time: on the wrong day. Wednesday. . . . What are the characteristics of Wednesday that make it improbable that James would agree to go drinking with Philip? On Wednesday is *Coronation Street*. Research shows that 36 per cent of the population watches *Coronation Street* on a Wednesday. Which indicates that there is a 3:7 chance that James stays in on Wednesday and watches *Coronation*

Street, and would therefore be unlikely to make a drinking date with Philip. Except that James has no television, and has never been known to visit other households to watch it. And even if he did or had, he might have forgotten either or both or the programme itself when he agreed to drink with Philip. Wedn'sday. WedNE Sday. WednesDAY. WEDnesday; semantic saturation: one might as well say Hip Hooray!

A cat inspects Philip, amorphous through laurel leaves. A lace curtain swings down. A passer-by shows by a minute change in his facial expression, that he knows of Philip's dark desire to rape and murder Mrs Druggett. A tall lover and his tiny lass pass by fantastically entwined: 'This is the monstrosity in love, lady, that the will is infinite and the capacity confined.' Why do those in buses look hurriedly away?

Here's a cop!

Go down three steps on to pavement. Go three paces east. Stop. Did the bell ring? A doggy is peeing on the wheel of somebody's status symbol. Queer look from bowler hat. Enact pantomime of sudden recall. Exaggerated about turn forefinger in air. Four purposeful steps west decline into a casual loiter. Stop. Surely even James. . . . Back. Up three steps. Laurel cat fascinated. Bowler hat titillated. Heel-bone grinding stone. Standing that long? Better go.

Turning, the angle between the grey plane of his face and the blue plane of the door, increased more rapidly than experience had led him to expect. Drunk? Exhaustion? Door moving? No!

'Will you come in?' said James, 'or shall we go straight to the pub?'

Oh Philip! for evidence on which to base your reply.

Well we have played our tape to the group, and suffered and enjoyed embarrassment and excitement, and have masked it all in our various ways.

'What on earth it has to do with *teaching*, beats me,' says one. And another, 'It's all quite fun, but think of those classrooms we have to return to next week. Think of the struggle *we* had to make the tape and compare our docile cooperative behaviour with the thirty-five second formers you may have been thinking of using the idea with.'

To get closer to what is educationally jargonized as 'the classroom situation', we have also had a 'creativity session', including all the English students, not just our limited group. It had been organized by one of the other groups and the room where it took place was littered with stimuli. Alarm clocks, pictures, collages, back numbers of glossy colour supplements, photographs taken from all kinds of magazines.

We were to choose our idea, work in groups and write – the tutors were to join in too.

At this particular session my creative spirit (or whatever) was in full flight – and by flight I mean retreat. Looking at the photographs which my group had ended up with, of splendidly (creatively?) wizened old peasants being herded by smooth cheeked American soldiers, I could only grin in a strained tooth-baring way and pass sardonic comment on everything.

When the time came for reading out our end-products our group was simply edgy and cross, and had produced nothing. We listened with faint sneers to the other contributions – solemn denunciations of war – high-minded exhortations to love and understand.

But Annette, who I had seen giggling with a group of girls in the corner, had found a response to the session which, in a way, justified it while puncturing its pretentiousness.

She had turned her Vietnamese misery over, and on the back she had discovered an advertisement for paint. It consisted of a grid of photographs of twenty-five front doors, all painted in different colours. The bottom right hand one was open, and on the steps sat a huge and hairy dog.

When her turn came, she went to the front of the room, showed us the picture, which made us all giggle nervously, and started to read in a caricature 'little-girl' voice.

'In my picture there are twenty-five doors. They are all painted different colours. One is red, one is pink, one is grey, one is. . . . Outside the open door is a lovely hairy dog called Bonzo.'

Now the reaction to this was very interesting. Annette has been rather out on a limb in our group, and she has remained unconvinced by the Institute ethos. I thought therefore that I could sense some irritation that she was not playing the right game over creativity. Certainly the laughter had an edge to it.

But look at it in the classroom. It is just the kind of reaction one might well get (as was mine of not writing at all). But it was more complex than that. And more creative too, if you like, because she had made a dramatic incident which expressed her reaction to the total context in which she was asked to 'be creative'. The implications of what she did reflected on and criticized, just as creative work should do, the very cherished bases of the educational posture of the Institute. That is not destructive; it is illuminating. I wished I'd thought of a similar solution to my predicament.

Be all that as it may, it's back to school on Monday!

Extract from teaching diary

I intend to devote most detail in this term's diary to a comparison between two first forms which are parallel and unstreamed, and two fourth forms. One of the fourths is T4 . . . bottom set early leavers, the other is 4E1, top set potential university people.

T4: I had our group tape copied by one of the Institute's technicians and I played it to them. Unfortunately, it had been copied at such low volume that they couldn't hear a thing if they sat in their seats. So we all collected in a heap on top of the tape recorder in one corner of the room.

They were interested in a way though the point we thought the tape had was entirely lost. They asked, 'Is that you, sir?' when they thought they recognized a voice. They missed the fine irony of our placing of the Beatles singing *He's a real nowhere man,* because they didn't notice the connection with the incident that preceded it. In any case the Beatles, pop in general, has a social significance. As soon as they recognized it they started to chat.

'I don't think it's as good as . . .'

'Oh I do. And I ought to know 'cos I've bought them both.'

'So have I.'

Etc.

Anyway after this inauspicious beginning they were so relaxed by the time the tape was over that the rest of the lesson was a dead loss. They had been most prepared to

listen to the comic elements – the poetry they totally
ignored. And they seemed to want to be merely amused for
the rest of the lesson.

Tuesday L6A: First lesson on the poetry of the 1930s. I
tried giving them a taste of the communist-polemic stuff.
We read six poems and their reaction was flat and
uninterested. They seem to have no curiosity about a new
book; perhaps they are surfeited. Even Louis MacNiece's
Bagpipe Music caused no excitement.

It's no go the government grants it's no go the elections,
Sit on your arse for fifty years and hang your hat
on a pension.

We got a snigger or two over 'arse', but no more. And
surely the idea is relevant? It's an idea they should find
some point in. In cosy subtopian Hershamfleet
particularly. Or are they all so full of acceptance of a
vaguely common-sensical socialism that they can't ask
any questions about what they are doing? I would have
thought that, as the A-level malaise begins to take hold,
they would have begun to ask themselves exactly that kind
of question. And with a general election announced
yesterday, and a brand new college of further education
just down the road, and with the prospect of government
grants and state scholarships just around the corner. And
so on. . . . But Mr Felton and Mr Purnell say they find this
bunch immovably dull too.

T4: Have started to write our conversations between two
people who do not know one another. I am highly dubious
about the results which I am banking on for Thursday
when Michael Cohen is coming to observe. I have asked if
some of them will be prepared to act them in front of the
class when he comes. They are so pleasant and friendly,
but they really do seem to be too relaxed. Roger and John
as a Pakistani door-to-door salesman and a housewife were
certainly hilarious. But at what level? What sort of
progress does it represent, if any?

What about teachers, then? I said in my first official diary entry
that Mr Felton was almost unbelievably helpful. And I meant it

and I mean it still. But, but, but ... but what? I feel that he approves of me because of what he imagines I am doing, not because of what I actually do. I cannot imagine him approving of T4 as they sat all over the desks chatting and smiling round the tape recorder. It is as though there were some line of toleration of the children which he manages to project into their minds, and over which they do not step. Why not? How do they know? Has someone tried it in the past and did he explode? With 1Z he manages to have them eagerly seeking his approval over things which I would consider trivial or boring. How does that happen? Does he carry an aura of authority by virtue of his position? But 'head of the English Department' cannot mean much to the children, surely.

And when I have seen Mrs Blake with T4, they are respectful and orderly, and she is clearly interested in what they have to say, and amused by the comments of Roger and John, but they say to me that they cannot stand her and she is a snob.

With that bunch it is extraordinary how they view propriety in the matter of who they can talk about and when. The other day they were having a general moan about school, and it was all becoming rather personal. They were frankly complaining about a number of members of staff, particularly about Mr Francis the new senior master, and they were cheerfully mentioning all their victims (or enemies) by name. I was in a sweat about it and was trying to put in a good word for the teachers, when in walks the head of Chemistry to collect some books from a cupboard. I confidently expected that they would tactfully change the subject, but no. They totally ignored the interruption and went blundering on with their outspoken condemnations. I suppose it is a tribute to the general prevalence of good sense at Hershamfleet, that there have been no repercussions.

They're quite right about Francis, he's a sod.

Extract from teaching diary

1Z: I have started project work with them on predators. They really enjoyed the idea. In the second lesson they

brought in masses of pictures and reference books of their
own and started compiling books and folders. The word
'predators' appears all over the place together with a steady
accretion of significance, factual, emotional, pictorial.
(Why does the project idea fall so flat with the older
forms?) I spent forty minutes this morning walking round
a room which was fairly buzzing with activity. Compare
the atmosphere generated by vocabulary and grammar
exercises last term. Does the instinct of curiosity get
diverted by the normal school programme, so that by the
fourth form (let alone the sixth) there is a division between
those things which arouse curiosity on the one hand, and
everything that happens in school, on the other? But with
L6A there seems to be no area which will arouse their
interest. The cosmos is equivalent to the A-level syllabus
and is inconceivably drab.

1X: But having said all that about the marvels of 1Z, what
about 1X? They would do no work at all. Perhaps there is
some kind of a critical balance. If more than a certain
proportion of a group want to work and know what they
are about . . . O.K. If less, then you've had it.

L6A: Have tentatively agreed to write for me. Not lit. crit.
but something else. It may be mere politeness, of course.

4E1: This is the top-stream lot about which John Purnell
was so enthusiastic. On his recommendation I read them
To women as far as I'm concerned, by D. H. Lawrence.
'The feelings I do not have I do not have', etc. They said
almost nothing . . . they just stared at me and refused
communication. I do not understand John's enthusiasm
. . . they were like L6A. Obviously intelligent and damned
dull at the same time.

T4: With Michael Cohen observing. I have never seen
those tough nuts being *coy* before! I wonder if my own
nervousness communicated itself to them. Still, when they
got around to talking they were very entertaining. But they
have not really got focused on anything yet. I can feel
myself relying on their friendliness – simply on a pleasant

informal kind of chit-chat – to see me through my four
weeks without too much difficulty.

1X: Were bloody. The difference between these two first
forms is astonishing. But then it may be that the project is
wrong (the subject is 'Night') or the time is wrong or . . .
or? It can't be entirely me if I can get on so well with 1Z.
(Can it?)

So what can the differences between these first forms be? Possibly
some sociological research would reveal something. From what I
know to be the case, though, there is a big difference in the way
their English teachers approach them.

1Z and Mr Felton, I have already described to some extent.
Although he does things with that form which *I* would consider
boring or trivial, he makes it clear that he respects them. His
towering figure in the classroom surrounded by their miniature
compact forms signals over this contrast of scale a concern for
the children.

Mrs Barker, on the other hand, signals desperation. She is no
schoolmarm with bun and moustache. She has wispy grey hair
and a curiously double face. The lines and folds which one
minute can be read as kindly, motherly, dullness, turn in a
moment into moralizing harshness which seems driven by fear. It
is not a moralizing that draws on strength and depth; it throws
out attitudes to bar the intrusion of the unknown.

Perhaps this means that when I, all unsuspecting, ask to see the
unknown, 1X must throw the lot at me?

It is strange seeing Michael Cohen in the Hershamfleet staff-
room. There is much polite bonhomie between him and Mr
Felton, some 'Did you know . . . ?' about former students who
had received their joint guidance, and some 'Have you read . . . ?'
about recent publications. I am too nervous to observe this very
clearly. I catch myself wondering how well they know one
another, and trying to imagine how they talk about me when I'm
not there. There is one thing – they don't have much time!

Michael was very good at fitting into the classroom with T4.
He seemed to give off the right sort of odour. The kids sniffed the
atmosphere and reckoned he was all right. If they were put off

their usual jolly manner it was probably more because of my tension than his presence. He offered to go out of the room when they were having trouble starting off their dialogues between strangers, but several voices said: 'No, no, 's all right,' or 'C'mon Roger, gerron wiv it.' Still, there is something deeply disturbing about having someone observing a lesson and pretending he's not there. It just does not work. The whole balance of the room is skewed, I think. Are there some people who can just carry on as though nothing were changed?

Extract from teaching diary

Monday

1Z: were just as industrious. Michael Cohen, who was observing, mentioned that they were all involved in discursive-type work – how, he asked, were they to be moved in the direction of imaginative writing? How could they be made to explore their attitudes to the animals? To cruelty? To killing? And so on. I am therefore going to try to use drama. Get them to act out stalking, seeing the prey, shooting. Reacting to dead animals. Being animals which are being hunted, are paralysed with fear, hiding, trusting in camouflage. Then we will see what happens in the writing.

L6A: I read their own reflections on 'Poetry of the Thirties' to them. Some had chosen poems which they clearly did not understand. Marilyn, for example, chose Dylan Thomas's *I have longed to move away*. I am uncharitably certain that she simply likes 'longing'.

T4: They are still chewing over their idea for a play in a disorderly rabble. Yesterday they improvised the lads in the cafe. It was very dull until someone suggested that the vicar should come in and attempt to be friendly. Today they were thinking about possible events which might have led up to or followed on from this incident. I would say that most of them talked or wrote on the subject for about five minutes out of the forty. I am very worried by the general disorderliness of the lessons, and the lack of any apparent results. To one side of this worry I am constantly nervous of being overlooked by other members of staff. I have no conviction in this lot!

Wednesday

1Z: Miming the predators idea in the hall. They were almost alarming in their involvement in the animal characters. When they started hunting they bared their teeth, and snarled and growled and tore with clawing fingers at the parquet floor. I was slightly surprised at their willingness to throw themselves into the idea. They clearly enjoyed it – what were they learning?

1X: Are problematical. It was the last lesson of the day and I asked them to do some writing. They reacted in their characteristic manner, by leaping about and shouting. I would have thought that nothing was achieved by this lesson. There was too much chaos, I would have said, there was too much fighting. But some of the kids offered me their work at the end of the lesson, 'would you like to read this, sir?' (they were not the goody-goodies who did this – they had been writing with one hand and thumping their neighbour with the other). And the work seemed to me to be very good.

For example: from *Fear at Night*

And the silence. I think, when lying awake at night, that the whole world has died in its sleep, so deep and still is that silence. A creak on the stairs and my hair stands on end, goose pimples rise on my neck. I tell myself there is nothing there in fact. I know the stairs are deserted. Then a car drones out of the distance and makes shadows on my wall and the oppressive silence is broken. But soon it is back again, an almost liquid silence which encompasses you and keeps you from sleeping.

Or from a panoramic view of night which included a scientist's view, a policeman's view and this *Poet's view.*

Poets take a very beautiful poetic view of night. They can make poetry up about nocturnal animals or to the moon.

Here is a poem I have made up.

The moon moves silently across the sky;
In the darkness an owl will fly,
While the cat prowls around
Observing all with his luminous eye.

The moon bathes the land with an unearthly glow
And all other prowling cats know
That this is the time the humans sleep,
So round dark alley ways they silently creep.

To poets then, night is a time when strange things and silent things go on.

Delightful stuff – and coming straight from chaos.

My next entry in my official diary begins: 'I funked having Mr Felton into this lesson.' I suppose I am lucky to have a choice about this. He always asks if I would like him to come and look; he puts it that way.

It is not just that I am nervous, like when playing in a concert. Whenever I think 'I am going to be observed,' I panic. I immediately decide that my normal way of going about things will not do for this occasion. What was I going to do?

A. I was going to walk in at the door.

NORMALLY. Two or three or four kids would wander towards me to pass the time of day – to comment on my tie – to show me some work – to make some cheeky-familiar remark. And normally I would be experimenting with honesty in my response. I would be seeing whether I could talk with them.

WITH AN OBSERVER. I would reach the blackboard much more quickly. I would avoid the eyes of the approaching children and mutter with no conviction 'go to your places please'. If they did so it would be on account of the authority aura of the observer.

Then:

B. I was going to talk about the drama session and suggest ideas for imaginative writing, poems, stories and so on.

NORMALLY. My eyes would be seeking the children's eyes

and I would be testing their movements and tensions, their kinds of listening. And I would be experimenting with their interruptions, and wondering why Lesley said this and Anne that.

WITH AN OBSERVER. The determinants of my linguistic choices would be largely conditioned by what I imagined the observer would be thinking of what I said. After all that is what he is there to see, to look at, observe.

Then:
C.

NORMALLY. I would say 'OK, please write,' and I would move about savouring that curious atmosphere which 1Z produce when they are working. I would talk to individuals: chat with ones who were bored: be interrupted by ones who had finished something and wanted me to read it.

WITH AN OBSERVER. I would lose patience through fear. I would be unable to listen to what this kid was saying because I had noticed that *that* kid had pulled out a comic and I wondered what the observer would think that had to do with predators.

Through all this is guilt and a sense of my inadequacy. I don't want people to see me teach. It is private. But why?

Extract from teaching diary

Monday

1Z: I funked having Mr Felton into this lesson as I wished to move away from factual to imaginative writing and I was not sure how they would take it. In the event I need not have worried. They reacted with their usual energy. The speed of their reaction amazes me. After ten minutes they were coming up with poems and insisting that I read them there and then. At the end of the lesson I said something vague like, 'if any of you have some work which you would *like* me to see, could you bring it to me now'. I was inundated with books and papers filled with writing and drawing.

Leslie Wollaston has done forty-three pages, part factual, part story, ranging from tigers to whales to prehistoric animals, and I haven't spoken more than two words to him for a fortnight. I remember complimenting him on a fine drawing of a tiger (on page 3) and before that I recall that he cracked some jokes at my expense when I asked him if he had any books about birds.

'Yeah,' he said.

'Well, perhaps you could make some drawings of birds of prey, showing beaks, claws, flight plans.'

'Oh! they're not about *that* kind of bird . . .'

T4: In the hall. Roger's play. This was not a success. But more through lack of cooperation than anything else. They seem not to be able to subordinate a desire to clown incessantly, to the business of making a dramatic improvisation emerge as something other than incessant clowning. Not surprisingly, the fight was the best bit!

L6A: Benskin, who in the A-level English lessons has done nothing but stare into the distance and stretch his long legs, and who, if he says anything at all works some kind of a sneer into it, has given me this poem to read.

Is it his own experience? or an imaginative extension of it? And does it explain his distant stare, perhaps?

Unconsummate

'I love you,' and with a straight face;
Her eyes held mine in a look of love and hope,
Of trust and devotion.
The hair of a brunette lay tumbled on the pillow
The arms on my shoulders,
The hands on my nape told me
She wanted me to stay – and for ever –
The warmth of our bodies and the
Soft of the bed told with her perfume
on my senses.
I could do nothing but kiss her and
Hold her to me. I gave her her wish
And I half believed. In her embrace
I felt free, and at rest, and . . .
In love.
She was with me; she had told me

And given me no mean assurance
That she was mine.
And yet I felt her plump thighs
And saw in her eyes the blindness
Of the young and innocent, and realized
Her helpless love reflecting mine.
I think she knew at the end that I
Did not love her as she loved me.
And that I used her only as my shelter
When the storm raged high and I,
Shipwrecked, swam gratefully under.
In her eyes I could see what I knew
Had once been me and what would
Never, never again; and I knew I longed for it.
But how could I break this child?
How could I tell in second-hand words?
Could I walk away? Run? or hide?
'Bide your time my darling, it's not yet nine.'

Wednesday

1Z: Here is some more relief from my maundering
pensées, in the form of some writing on predators.

    Nicholas, from *Killed by Superior.*

Man is superior to beast because he has weapons with which to
kill; guns, arrows, knives. But then you say – well, beasts have
weapons too. Sharks have razor sharp teeth, and long ones at
that. A rhino has speed and a terrible horn.

    An animal can only get man if he has an advantage. Behind
him, near him, when the man has no weapon, or is too scared to
use it.

    So animals turn to smaller creatures than themselves, who in
turn are killed by superior.

    Elaine had made some notes about scorpions and some
charming drawings of them. Rather plump and friendly
scorpions in the drawings. Here is his poem:

Me Scorpion

1. Me Scorpion,
   Deadly enemy of the tarantula:
   Sting-pack resting in my back;

I sense the forthcoming of him,
Him the TARANTULA,
He stands, still as night;
Cold-blooded, crafty and wicked.

2. The battle commences,
He corners me,
No, no I get free,
Again, I'm clear.
Cornered, he comes closer.
I must die either way.
The black scorpion digs its sting pack
    into its own back.
        Death!

The lower sixth are *very* curious people. L6A, they are called.
And that is supposed to denote the brightest and best of the
youth of Hershamfleet. They are so *boring*. Felton and Purnell
say they find the same. They sit like toads in cold rows waiting
for my instructions. No matter how brilliant and provocative
that instruction is, they allow themselves no flicker of response. I
feel they are watching each other; they are bored with every word
I say; they make a note of something because anxiety about the
exam just, and only just, overcomes inertia.

What the hell are they doing here? I ask myself.

What the hell is education all about if these characters, so
highly selected, so groomed for the upper echelons and all that
crap, are so bored by it? So totally, so foggingly, so paralysingly
dead to Shakespeare, to Hardy, to the 'Poetry of the Thirties'.

I mean that. They paralyse me. I feel if I stop saying things it
will take several minutes for them to recognize that that has
happened. Gradually they will become irritably aware that their
ecology has subtly altered. Silence, the absence of the school-
masterly mutter, will filter through like a change in temperature
and they will shift their cold reptilian haunches and stare re-
proachfully toad-eyed at me until I begin again.

Michael Cohen says they have had their curiosity trained out
of them; that they understand that success comes from quiet
orderly acceptance. He says I should try doing something totally
different with them and has lent me a tape of his called *Ado-*

lescents on Adolescence. It is a collection of writing by pupils of his.

I'm prepared to try anything.

Extract from teaching diary

Tuesday

L6A: I played them Mr Cohen's tape *Adolescents on Adolescence.* An interesting reaction.

'We're going to look at some pieces of writing by people of your own age.'

Bustle of enthusiasm. As they listened and read they were very interested, but their explicit comments were rather snooty. They were (naturally?) rather unwilling to admit that they felt *with* the pieces though there was some grudging praise offered. They liked the piece called 'on being faced with a blank sheet of paper', though they said that they felt it was rather naïve to admit to such a passion for football. Sympathy with the writers was expressed cautiously in the past tense. They had felt like that once, they said, implying heavily that they had now grown out of it. They liked 'My love during the week', though they thought it was 'uneven'. They admitted being impressed by the honesty of the author when he said that as he held his girl-friend's hand he felt that he was somehow 'betraying his parents'. (How does that square up with Benskin's poem?) More tomorrow for the last lesson.

It certainly makes more impact than literature!

Wednesday

L6A: There are no more direct reactions to Mr Cohen's tape to record, really. The class was restive, seemed (as usual) bored, and when they watched a sparrow outside the window, trying to fly away with an enormous piece of cotton wool, I sympathized. And so we all watched it – it did seem so much more interesting and immediate than A-level – until it had torn off a small bit and flown away. I then asked them despairingly if they were fed-up with listening to the tape.

'No, no,' they cried in chorus, but in the silence that followed someone (I think it was Anne) said she was just fed-up generally. I said,

'How very interesting,' which being a fatuous mannerism of mine which they have noticed, made them laugh.

But that did not kill the topic because Anne picked it up with unwonted energy and embarked on a massive indictment of Hershamfleet. In general terms they feel they have a lot of work to do which does not offer them any satisfaction. They never feel they have completed anything. They cannot sit back for a moment and chat because they feel guilty. If they have a free lesson they *must* go to the library and work in silence. They are not allowed to go into one of the little rooms off the library and chat. Talk about work or simply talk and relax and postpone the homework until the evening.

Two of them were banned from the library for a week by Mr Francis, the deputy head. They had to work in the dining room instead.

'Big punishment!' said one.

Most of their free lessons coincided with junior lunch so they had to work in the library anyway. When they did work in the dining-room they could talk. There was no permanent supervision and therefore no absolute ban. So when the week was over they asked Mr Francis if they could work in the dining-room permanently during their free lessons.

'*Certainly not!*' he said, 'back you go to the library.'

Anne's timetable was not full enough this year, so she has to attend a series of lessons which she has no interest in.

When I asked 'Why?' she said, 'I was told, "it's *good* for you" – just like greens – so I go.'

Someone else said 'They (teachers) are always concerned with piffling little things like uniform.'

In the sixth form they can, in official theory, wear what they like. In practice it must have long sleeves, be a different colour, the skirt must be so long, etc., etc.

The A-level subjects, they say, are interesting enough, but too much fuss is made of them.

Mr Francis has somehow, in two terms of honest application to duty, made himself disliked throughout the school. T4, who are one of his favourite targets, despise him to a man; they call him little Hitler. The staff give each other significant shrugs and sighs when his name is mentioned, and some of them have found it necessary to 'explain' him to me. 'He doesn't understand about ...,' and 'He doesn't try to see that. ...' To me he seems a quiet, whispering fascist. His orders are gracelessly framed as requests. He asks you to take extra lessons – do this – do that – standing too close to you and staring to see if you flinch from his bad breath. He is small, peeled looking, and with his pale-blue pale-pink rimmed eyes, he ingratiatingly imposes on you.

Anyway, L6A seems to be alienated, and this, it seems, is the first time they have been collectively vocal about it. 'Golly, I thought it was just me,' they said. And, 'I didn't realize anyone else felt like that.' This seemed to me to be a good thing, and probably a tangential reaction to the tape. I hope that, by encouraging such a discussion I am not laying up trouble for other people who have to teach them. They *say* they have never liked going to school since half-way through their first year, when they stopped being excited by the fact of being at a new school. Most of them, on the other hand, remember enjoying primary school. This lesson was the first occasion on which I felt we had some common ground. Part of what made it possible, was the fact that Benskin and his squashing remarks were absent. Part was undoubtedly the sparrow. And part was the atmosphere engendered by the tape recording.

Intelligence seems such a useless concept when trying to sort out why L6A are like they are. Intelligent they certainly are, but this is a grammar school, so all the children are intelligent by one definition. L6A are also the successes of the school – the 'high fliers'. High flier is a head-masterly term, a chief education officer expression for speech days. It bears no imaginative relationship to these students, who go through school burdened and bound by their work. They do not give the impression of being released into some pure, clear, upper atmosphere of the intellect.

4E will be their successors in two years time and I think they show similar tendencies. They are quiet, orderly, attentive. How much quiet, orderly attentiveness can they take without concluding that success means orderly attention to the officially issued wisdom?

T4 are disorderly. That is the most striking difference between these two groups. It seems to be more a matter of the way they behave, than of their absolute capacity to understand things. It is as though there were a certain kind of behaviour towards adults which allows education to 'take'. And I find that kind of behaviour pretty dull, after all. I suppose some people would say that a lot of learning is just a hard, dull toil, and that one has to accept the fact. And perhaps there is some stoical virtue in accepting it – or there would be if it were really a fact.

In my next entry in the teaching diary I give accounts of two reactions to drama lessons. One is from Christine Ash of T4, the bottom set; the other from a group of boys in 4E, the top set. The differences are fascinating. Christine seems to take all the responsibility for T4's failure to make a play, onto herself and the others in the group. 4E, on the other hand, use the drama lesson as a means of pointing out the teacher's (i.e. my) failure to make an earlier English lesson work.

Extract from teaching diary

Thursday

T4: Christine writes about T4's attempt to make a play. The lesson in the hall was a riot but look at this criticism of it.

In the Hall with Mr Otty or
T4 trying to produce a play with Mr Otty

The play was a complete failure. No one knew what anyone else was doing. The other three girls and I were only told to walk in and sit at a table. We did this and a few minutes later four boys walked in. These four were talking so much that you could not hear what Roger and Tony were saying. Then when the vicar walked in his conversation went on too long with the boys. When they started fighting the boys got too carried away and they were larking about too much.

When the other three girls and I walked in we tried to get a conversation started but we were too quiet and no one paid any attention to us. After a few minutes on stage I lost complete interest in the play, and I was more interested in looking out at the people in the corridor. The only real bit of thinking and acting that was in the play (well this is what I think) was when Barbara was off stage and she shouted for more rolls. This brightened the play up for a minute or two, then it went dead and silent again.

I think it needs a lot more thought before T4 attempts to write and produce another play. All the boys and girls need to get together and add all their ideas. We need a sort of chairman to write all the ideas down. Then with these ideas a group of about four (two girls and two boys) need to get together and write the play. Then we need an introduction to the play telling the form exactly what the play is about. This should be read to the form and the people chosen for the different parts. Each person chosen for a part should be given a sort of script of the sort of things to say and when to say them. They need not learn these things, but they ought to know what to say and have these as a help if they dry up in the middle of a conversation. Then we need two or three practices before the play is put on the stage.

After that I think T4 ought to be able to produce a very good play (if they followed the above instructions), because we do have some talent in our form.

On second thoughts, perhaps, my ideas of how T4 can produce a play are hopeless, because I am too much of a dreamer to be able to do anything right.

The concrete suggestions are all her own. 'Dreamer', she says . . . but I can see Mrs Blake or Mrs Barker putting the word on her report. When I read the piece to the class they were amazed to find that someone was convinced there was talent in the form. The last paragraph seems to reflect a general attitude. Our education here teaches a fair slice of our top 18 per cent to expect and accept failure. Some other people wrote about the play business using what they

saw as a fiasco, as proof that such activities were too
difficult for T4.

Friday

4E: Drama in the hall. I suggested that they divide into
groups and improvise on a situation which contained two
elements who did not know one another. Interview for a
job – new teacher and class – etc.

The largest group did a very good take-off of my first
lesson with them. A quiet boy with a limp and a foxy
inquisitive face played the part of me. He wandered into
the class sheepishly to the suppressed giggles of the pupils
and wrote, as I had done, a poem on the board. Instead
of:

'The feelings I don't have I don't have . . .'
he wrote,
'What I don't know I don't know,
What I don't know I don't want to know.'
And so on.

Then he started asking the class what they thought about
it and, as I had done, he got no response. There was just
that silent watchfulness while he, as I had done, stammered
and groped for another way of asking the same fatuous
question.

In desperation he changed the subject. 'All right,' he
said, 'forget about the poem. Now what do you think about
the colour problem?' And so it went on.

Teacher: 'Well, what *do* you think about colour
prejudice? You must have *some* views on it, surely.'

At last there is a reply. The 'teacher' looks relieved and
then appalled as a pupil says in a strong, parody Pakistani
accent:

'Oh, yessir, I tink dey should send ol of dem wogs home,
dat's wot I tink, yes really.'

Teacher: 'Well, that's very interesting. Thank you. Now
what about the rest of you. Do you all agree with his
opinion?'

Silence. Teacher looks at his toes, shuffles across in front
of blackboard, frowns at the end of a piece of chalk.

Suddenly he looks up with a cunning smile. He has found
a new move.
Teacher: If no one agrees with him, does anyone
disagree?

Silence, and the watching momentarily broken by a
slight cough from one of the pupils.
Teacher: 'Yes? . . . I thought someone was going to . . . yes?
. . .' Pathetic eyebrow raised pleading for *some* response.
Same pupil as before, still in same strong Pakistani accent:
'Yessir, I definitely *dis*agree most strongly.'

Class and audience (and myself) fall about with
laughter. End of sketch.

It was a good critique of the lesson. After all when a
situation gets like that it is unstoppable. As soon as the
class has seen that the teacher wants a response of *any*
kind, that he is panicked by the silence, they become much
more interested in watching his strategies than in
discussing what he is asking them to respond to.

For my private record, to finish off this second crazy term (thank
God it is over) here are some pieces by my loony 1X. Still they
rush around, fight, scream and tear at my nerves and dig up my
guilt and my feelings of total defeat and inadequacy, and still
they turn out poems like these with a careless ease.

1. *Thoughts at night*

A fire might occur
While I'm asleep.
I'd be burnt at the stake
No chance to live.

The house might fall down.
What shall I do then?
I'd be covered with rubble.
No chance to live.

But I wake in the morning
Alive and gay
And laugh in scorn
At my thoughts at night.

2. A spatter of rain,
   On the wet pavement.
   A tread of feet
   On the wet pavement.
   A cigarette box dropped in a hurry
   On the wet pavement.
   The moon shines down
   On the wet pavement.
   Lovingly.

3. *The Nightwatchman*

   The nightwatchman finished his cup of tea.
   Then got up and had a look round.
   Nobody there.
   He sat down and smoked his pipe,
   Then threw the match in the fire.
   It flared up with an unearthly glow.
   He stood up and walked around.
   Nobody there.
   He turned and went into his hut,
   Slamming the door behind him.
   Nobody there.

   How do they evoke that stillness and isolation of night time in
the blaring chaos of my lessons? How on earth do they do it?

Summer term

It is one of the often repeated statements at the Institute that the 'big bang' exam is a failure as a means of assessment. All the arguments about the injustice to certain candidates who do not write well under pressure, about the irrational assumption that the ability to expound glibly and rapidly is desirable, about representing a year's study in a few three-hour papers, about the emphasis on memory and so on, come glibly and rapidly from every member of staff. So it is something of a jolt to realize that very soon we will all be scribbling off a few three-hour papers. This is all part of the current underground muttering in our tutorial group.

'Here we go again. Another morning wittering over creativity and spontaneity. Don't they realize we've got to write our damned exams in eight weeks' time.'

And so on.

But it is a pretty disastrous kind of anomaly. How are we expected to campaign vigorously in the schools for the abolition exams, or even for mode 3 CSE, if our authority to do such campaigning comes from our success in a typical old-fashioned exam?

In any case the teaching practice is at the beginning of this term, so either that or the exams will have to be relegated to a firm second place. And they are sending an external examiner to see one of my lessons: a thought that makes my knees go to jelly. It makes me wish very firmly that they'd stuck totally to written papers.

Extract from teaching diary

I wonder if my charming 1Z are heading, by virtue of their docile manners, for the top-stream, 4E, L6A, kind of freeze-up? Their work certainly has less bite than 1X's.

I've been doing 'Fire' with them this term, and this led

to a rather curious conversation with one of them. He wanted to do a story about being trapped by fire, but did not know how to begin. I just listened to what he had to say for a bit, and he demonstrated that he had taken all Mr Felton and I had said to heart.

'You see Mr Felton says it's best to write about things that have happened to you, and I've never been trapped in a burning house.'

Faced with this diminutive philosopher I was tempted to argue it all out explicitly about making connections and re-combining elements of one's experience to explore it, and deepen its significance. But there was a strange block in my mind too. It is not that explicitness of analysis could prevent good work, dry up creative springs or whatever, it was the way he saw analysis. As though he felt that the kind of thinking which leads to the conclusion: 'it is best to write from your own experience' were a teacherly kind of thinking – not *his* kind of thinking. He seemed to be waiting for my instructions before he could do what I wanted instead of taking his idea for the story and discussing how best to tackle it.

The project has not gripped them like predators did. Today's lessons did not hum with activity. Some wrote, some read and some just talked.

Here are some results.

Picture Poem

BLUE	SPARKS	HECTICALLY
ORANGE	BLAZES	BLUSHINGLY
RED	ARCS	FEVERISHLY
YELLOW	ROARS	STRONGLY
WHITE	FLASHES	QUICKLY
GREEN	SPRINGS	CHEMICALLY
AMBER	SMOKES	SLOWLY
ASHES	GLOW	SOFTLY
TOO MANY	FIRE ENGINES	TOO LATE

By Nigel
And,

The Flames of the Universe

The flames that ride the skyways in a ball of fiery heat, giving light and heat to nations of the planets of its reach.

It rages with the wrath of gods, the gods of war and heat, it burns with untold fury just unleashed, it fights the forces of space itself with a gaseous flaming force, of untold heat the sun is made a fiery burning source.

The flames that own the universe the nothingness of space, the far reaches of the meteors, it fills up all of space. The light, it owns the shadows, and controls them with great might. The heat it warms the peoples, to fufill its flaming plight.

This description of our light and heat is all I know to write, but for many reasons the flames that own the sun fulfill their endless plight.

by Peter

This second one is a curious piece. What does he mean by 'plight'? One could make sense of the thing by reading it as 'thing plighted', 'promise', 'pledge'. He seems to have been quite unconsciously inflated by the grand rum-te-tum of the rhythm of the Battle Hymn of the Republic.

I think I must try to get 1Z for my ordeal with the external examiner.

Why, for God's sake, didn't I refuse to be externally examined? I can't even think about it I'm so scared.

I try to bring my mind to bear on the problem and it immediately slides away from it. First, I'm sure that my usual way of going on in a classroom won't impress anybody. Second, I've never planned a lesson which went as I planned it. Third, there will be two almost total strangers in the room when it has to happen. Can't I arrange not to be there?

Getting a big grip. . . .

I SHALL: Take Nigel's picture poem as a starting point and try to build up word association meshes on the blackboard based on 'fire-heat' and 'ice-cold'. Then I shall tell them to get on with their projects and I shall skate about the room keeping my eyes averted from the examiners.

But it is next Tuesday that they are to come!

Extract from teaching diary

Friday

T 4: They are exactly as they were. Any effect which
Christine's criticism of the play might have had last term is
now entirely lost. They can't put off the delights of an easy
laugh, so we can't get anything off the ground. They want
to try, they say sometimes, but seriousness seems like a
betrayal of their social ethos. If only one could write the lot
off as useless, but Roger, John, Christine, Vanessa, they're
far too bright for that.

I gratefully accepted Mrs Blake's offer of a folk-song
broadcast to use with them, and now I wish I hadn't. It
really fed my prejudices. Genuine mouth music it was.
Hamish Macsporran, a nonagenarian gardener from
Craigellachie reedily chanting some incomprehensible ditty
about 'happing yer neaps frae the harr', and an ancient
crone from County Tyrone.

Monday

Lower Sixth, General English: This is a sample of abortive
discussion about music. I played them Webern's five pieces
for Orchestra Op. 10, really just to put before them some
new, different, sounds, which could neither be slotted into
the Beethoven pigeonhole nor into any of the pop
pigeonholes.

'I don't like it.'

'Oh.'

' 'S all right if you like that kind of thing.'

'Yes.'

Pause.

'Well, we have two more lessons before I leave you (sob,
sob, sniff, sniff) so what are we going to do in them?'

Pause.

'More music.'

'More music, all right. Have you, any of you, got any
records you could bring?'

'Yeah, *Aftermath.*'

T–LT–C

'Good, what about you? What sort of records do you have?'

'Load of old rubbish.'

'Oh . . .?'

'Well, that's to say, I think it's a load of old rubbish.'

'Well, why buy them?'

'My parents bought them'

'What's wrong with them?'

'They're dated.'

(When he says 'dated' does he mean the Inkspots or Rock around the Clock, or the Beatles, or what?)

'What about you, then?'

'Who, me?'

(I've panicked this one, he glances over his shoulder as though he could not believe his fate so evil that I should speak to him.)

'Yes. You. What sort of records do you have?'

'Er, what do you mean?'

(What on earth *do* I mean?)

'Well, you mentioned *Aftermath*.'

'Oh, yeah, but I didn't buy that.'

'Oh.'

'I was given it, see.'

(So what!)

'So . . .?'

Pause.

'And what about you?'

'Well, I bought my records some time ago, see. I wouldn't buy them now.'

And so on.

They are so firmly on the defensive that they look for an ambush in everything I say. The attack they expect and fear will be intellectual, anti-philistine, possibly with a class slant to it.

The examiners came to see me with 1Z today. They were all charm and smiles and reassurance as we strolled casually down corridors. I feel people are bound to notice my terror at moments like these. My gestures become stiff and jerky, my face freezes up and there is a harsh knocking in my temples. But they never do notice. They think I'm having an off day. They don't believe I'm just scared.

Well, in they come to the classroom. 1Z stands in unwonted and respectful and frankly inquisitive silence. The examiners sit at the back of the room on those tiny first-form chairs and squint at my teaching diary between them. They try hard not to be noticed. They look about as inconspicuous as Nelson's column. Trying to ignore their existence and get on with the job is like trying to ignore a ghost at a banquet.

'Take any shape but that' ... I should shout. I should express this terror.

But I rush to the blackboard so fast I almost hit the wall.

'Right, sit down. Quiet, QUIET!'

I try to make it all sound calm and friendly, but my voice is strangled and thin and dry. There is no saliva in my mouth or throat, and my tongue feels too big.

I attempt to explain about word association, and by the time my mind catches up with my mouth it is too late. I'm off, jabbering hard and dry, trying to find words that will reach 1Z and at the same time explain and excuse myself to the examiners. I achieve neither object. 1Z look puzzled and glance at each other in embarrassment. The tall lady and the tubby, grey gentleman at the back of the room frown at my feet and then smile at the ceiling and then glance at each other in embarrassment.

In a shaky, scarcely legible hand I scribble, 'Fire' on the blackboard and I jabber some more, and then suddenly I give up. I know it won't come right now. So with a grim grin I croak ...

'Right, carry on with your projects then ...' and I scamper nervously among the rows of desks trying to bring my exploding bouncing mind to concentrate on the children's questions.

I am disgusted that I should be so feeble. It is the same with auditions, concerts, even playing chamber music with new people. It is as though something deep inside me threw all these symptoms out to excuse my failure.

The examiners are so kind afterwards.

'We did enjoy the diary, it was *so* interesting,' says the gentleman. But the lady says, smiling all the while, 'I didn't quite follow what you were doing with the word-association idea. We must talk about it sometime.' And they depart to terrify someone else and leave me hollow and damp and gloomy.

An interview at Willowgrove school.

'Come in, come in ... Mr ... er ...' (glance down at my application forms on the desk) ... 'Mr Otty. Good, well, you seem to have the right kind of qualifications. Now, would you like to have a glance at this programme from our last speech day while I make some notes here? Eh? Good.'

He presses a buzzer and a curious little hatch at my back slides open. A head bobs out of it making me jump.

'Ah. Miss Tomkins, the file on Brown, 3G. Thank you, thank you. Large comprehensives, Mr Otty' (he twinkles kindly eyes through steel-rimmed spectacles) 'they seem to be all administration.'

He gives me a further five minutes to take in his short, stout but immaculate figure, his crisp grey hair and crisp grey suit, and his surprisingly youthful, rather too well defined, pink lips. He shifts and fiddles and adjusts his gown and my eyes whip back to the speech-day programme.

'Well, what do you think of it?'

'What are these prizes for integrity and loyalty?'

'Oh I suppose it is the kind of thing they tend to emphasize more in public schools, Mr Otty. You know the kind of case. Every year there are some boys or girls in the school who, though they do not attain any academic distinction, and aren't any good at games, are nevertheless the salt of the earth, and I feel – I instituted those two prizes myself – that they should not be left out at speech day.'

'Sort of booby prizes for nice chaps?'

'Yes, er' (another glance at my application forms on the desk). 'Yes you could say that, I suppose.'

Some time later, 'I beat them y' know. The girls too; they respect me for it.'

And, after another half hour, 'You'll find the staff a happy one. They are entirely united, they all hate me.'

At coffee I discover the truth of this remark. All the interviewees are advised only to come to the school if they can stand up to a loony headmaster. It is the obsessive topic of conversation. They all discuss him all the time. How he interferes, how he annoys, how he makes trouble among the kids, how tyrannical, how inconsistent he is.

After break we see the school. The purpose-built buildings, the foundations of the new drama studio, the site of the new sixth-form centre. And we are warned about how to behave at lunch.

This meal is a ludicrous cross between public school and comprehensive. The children sit in groups of six at round tables. The emphasis there is on informality and social interchange. The staff and interviewees file in to a refectory high table, gowns billowing, faces stern. We wait silently while the head does a solo entrance and says a Latin grace.

In the afternoon we again form an embarrassed group outside the head's room. Noises of school surround us. Raised and hectoring voices. Scraping chairs. And the senior master with huge feet, and acres of black gown, strides about the corridor sometimes shouting at and sometimes grabbing at passing pupils. A noisy, blundering, violent man, he suddenly transforms all this into an ingratiating stoop and murmur as he talks to the head round the edge of the door.

I am summoned for another forty-five minute session.

'I don't interfere, y' know. I trust my teachers so long as they deliver the goods. English teachers must get the children through their exams, and that means they must teach spelling, punctuation, grammar. Grammar is the foundation of a sound style.'

I resist a temptation to lay my head back and shout 'Balls!'

'With the greatest respect,' I say, 'we seem to talk different languages as far as English teaching goes.'

'Go on.'

I go on. I mention 'creative' work.

'Oh yes, we have lots of that here. Have you seen our magazine? But, take a tip from an old hand, it mustn't interfere with the real work. You'll see.'

Then he tells me to wait outside. The senior master arrives among us and says, 'Nobody who wants the job is to leave. Mr Tickle says it may take all evening but he must see you all again.'

At my final session the head stands with my application in his hand and points his little belly at the wall on my left. He moves his head slowly round until he can stare at me over his left shoulder. Suddenly he whips his glasses off and narrows his eyes.

'Mr Otty, if I offered you the job of head of my English department, would you take it?' He pops the glasses back on and raises interrogative eyebrows. (Will each candidate be treated to this pantomime?)

'No,' I say.

'Go on.'

'I have no experience of how to run an English department in a huge comprehensive school. Also I have told you that I don't agree with corporal punishment, that I think your speech-day programme is phoney, and that we totally disagree about how English should be taught. We should be constantly fighting, Mr Tickle.'

'But I don't want yes-men on my staff! I've been a socialist, a radical, all my life. I'm not a yes-man myself. My governors do exactly what I tell 'em to do.'

But he did not offer me any kind of a job, so I am spared the agony of a decision.

The complaints about the exams came out into the open. Michael Cohen said it usually did by this stage in the year, and he apologized for the Institute's exam system. And then he pointed out something that interested me a great deal.

'If you set up a post-graduate certificate course, exams are anyway pretty redundant. If the students are post-graduate they have been selected by a most gruelling series of exams from age eleven onwards. You lot,' he gestured round the room, 'are by definition among the best exam-passers in the world.'

It made me look at exam-passing in a new way – as a technique independent of the subjects examined. After all, all one has to do is to look at the situation, see what they want, see what one has, see the most economical way of letting them have it.

In this spirit I am approaching these exams with a slightly contemptuous confidence. I know what work I have to do and I know I have time to do it. Only occasionally do the old superstitious heeby-jeebies creep up behind me with childhood words like 'swank'.

Extract from teaching diary

My teaching diary is rather thin this term. Never mind I can blame it all on the exams. Here, anyway, is one final extract on 1X.

In the end they turned up trumps again. None of the work was quite as good as some last term. But the quantity of stuff, all done in rough and improved on for the final version, is staggering. Even Lyndon produced *something*. He had done it in his own time, at home, presumably so that he could devote the entire lesson to the exercise of his disruptive talents.

A fascinating insight into Mark. He produced no work again. I had assumed that he was clever, imaginative usually troublesome. In fact I gather he is not thought bright, he is always 'poor' in imaginative work, but in Mrs Barker's formal lessons he does very careful neat work on set problems. He must have been completely lost in the atmosphere of 1X projects. All my efforts to interest him in imaginative suggestions, must have made him worse. On the other hand he showed a kind of destructive initiative and imagination in the endless schemes he devised to prevent other people working and to drive me insane.

1X have a group joke about a beast called 'Scraggy-cat'. This kept on cropping up in the middle of serious work on the fire topic.

For example:

Some Equations
CAT + fire = (unknown matter)
Ashes + unknown matter = burnt cat
Ashes + unknown matter − fire = cat
Cat + fire − unknown matter = ashes.

And this:

Scraggy
Scraggy drank some acid
Which burnt him all inside,
He tried to drink an alkali
Hoping that they might collide

If an acid and an alkali do meet
It is proved of the burning, it will cease,
Poor old scraggy didn't last that long
So, they let him Burn. In. Peace.

Very strange, I reckon.

Interview at Grove End Grammar school.

At Willowgrove school I talked for over two hours with the headmaster. We really discovered things about each other, and, with good reason, he did not offer me the job. At Grove End after fifteen or twenty minutes of cautious non-communication I was appointed.

I really don't know what the point of the interview was. Miss Prynne simply frowned down at my letter of application, and said,

'I see you read English at Cambridge, is that right?'

'Yes.'

'Good,' another downward squint, 'and at present you are at the Institute?'

'Yes.'

I fully expected that she would go on to verify my age, as though she were trying to uncover some discrepancy between my answers now and the factual content of my letter.

The head of the English department was more communicative. He particularly suggested that I should not worry too much about the buildings. These are an astonishing collection of drab wooden barrack rooms opening off a corridor which is geometrically straight, about a quarter of a mile long, and rather smelly. It was a hospital during the First World War and the school was started here as a 'temporary' measure in the 1920s. It makes one aware how little people mean when they talk piously about the importance of education. A valued institution in a wealthy community is not housed for over forty years in lousy temporary accommodation. Forty years! That takes one almost half-way back to the 1870 Education Act!

The educational psychology tutor asked our group today if we could apply any of our new knowledge and experience to criticize the teaching methods at the Institute.

We immediately told her what she must have known already,

how we spent our Friday mornings. There can be nothing more 'teacher-centred' than sitting several rooms away from the teacher, hearing his pearls of wisdom crackling through a loud-speaker system. And, we went on, there can be few things more crudely ironical than that the content of lectures delivered in this fashion should be concerned with involving the learner in the educational process, with pupil-centredness and with avoiding the cold formality of the lecture-type lesson.

Was she acting when she rounded her eyes, complimented our perspicacity and said, 'that's a *very* good point'?

I have written my exams with a roaring hubristic confidence (very different from the practical!) but when people ask me how they went, I say:

'Oh, I *think* they were all right.'

At University I was highly motivated to succeed, but was entirely at a loss as to how to do it. To begin with, I tried very hard to work, but most of it seemed meaningless and much of the rest appeared pointless, and I refused to admit the former, and my questions about the latter were not taken seriously. I felt under very strong pressure not to betray my ignorance, not to let people know that I had never looked at Piers Plowman and had never heard of Leavis. I failed to read *From Ritual to Romance* because the first time I heard of it was when my medieval tutor referred to it as something which I would, of course, have already read. I felt the book was so obviously important to English students that I dared not even admit to librarians or shop assistants that I did not possess it. In my mind I saw myself nonchalantly strolling into Bowes & Bowes and saying as I asked for a copy 'I've lost my own one,' or 'it's for a present, you see,' but I never managed it.

My teachers put all this down to laziness, to not taking the work seriously; they were entirely wrong, but I accepted, in the end, their authoritative classification. Really, I suppose, I gave up thinking about it. When I thought about remedying the situation I thought in terms of spending more time on my work. When that failed to do any good I quickly dropped the idea in case I was forced to conclude that I was simply too stupid to succeed.

Some senior members of the University clearly felt that it would be impertinent of them to mention work to me at all. They assumed that I had decided to have an easy time, a gay social life, and to scrape a degree of some kind. Since I preferred to be thought cavalier than stupid, I lived up to this reputation in a mild kind of way. The famed tutorial system was an intellectual gossip shop for me. I would read my essay, the tutor would quite rightly see nothing of value in it and quite wrongly assume that that was the way I liked it, so he offered round drinks and we chatted about little known and scurrilous details of the private lives of famous literary names.

A sinologist who stood *in loco parentis* for me, suggested I go and see a psychiatrist, he knew *such* a nice one, he said. When I showed indignation he dropped the idea immediately.

One is bound to feel respect for the traditions of research which are maintained at our ancient universities. Even if a lifetime of dedicated industry throws up no more than an emendation or two to the text of the *Aeneid*, one can't help admiring that dedication. But nevertheless should not an educational institution take more interest in the intellectual development of the less brilliant students? There was talk about 'spoon feeding' being a bad thing, but that argument is based on such a crude and inadequate model of learning, that it surely cannot have been seriously proposed. Perhaps they saw the whole function of the university in different terms which made the problems I am raising here disappear or at least shrink. Perhaps the idea was that so long as they got their tiny quota of highly trained brilliance, then they were happy that the rest should form a balanced community of over-privileged losels, loblollymen and louts?

I am grateful to the Institute, therefore, because it does attempt to live up to the implications of its expressed intentions. Here they seem to have some central purpose backed by some central insight about which they care sufficiently deeply to want to share it with the students they admit. In my corner of Cambridge it seemed to be assumed that you would share the basic values of the place with its oldest inhabitants. If you did not, that was too bad, there were plenty who did, and the values were too self-evidently sanctioned by prestige and antiquity to need justifying to every little pipsqueak of an undergrad.

Part Two
The Probationary Year

Autumn term

Well here I am at Grove End School. I am writing this in the staff room which is without exception the most squalid place I have ever entered. The lino on the floor is institution green – or was institution green before it was charred with cigarettes, torn by chair legs and heels, and irregularly varnished with a mixture of tea and coffee, cigarette ash and chalk dust. The chairs are an amazing collection of rejects and relics from wartime NAAFIs with springs poking through and broken arms and cigarette burns and more stains from tea and coffee. The tables round the wall are several feet thick in ancient yellowed exam papers and roneoed notes and report forms and battered textbooks. The wooden walls have been painted piecemeal, but surely not since the last war, so there is a patchwork effect of greys and yellows all of which were once supposed to be white. The knots of the wooden boards show through the paint dappling it a darker grey.

In the centre is a sticky formica-topped table where the coffee and tea are placed at break, and above it hanging from the rafters by a piece of grubby string, swings the staff's sticky and corroded teaspoon.

The staff sit in three irregular but immutable circles in a row down the narrow length of the room. I tend to stand most of the time, but there is a circle to which most of the new staff clearly belong.

The day before term began, Mr Curle called a staff-meeting. He welcomed the new members of staff by reading their names out from a list. Then he handed copies of this list to all members of staff (it turned out to be a staff list showing people's names and the forms they were to take charge of) and then when we could all see it he proceeded to read it aloud to us. I had a feeling that this was pointless at the time, but in a new institution it is difficult to judge the significance of its rituals.

He then made a statement of policy about exams. The school, he indicated, was not primarily concerned with how many people it got through the external exams. It recognized that there were more important aspects of education to consider, and so on. And then for an extinguishingly boring forty-five minutes he proceeded to spout about who had passed what, and what the percentage pass was overall, and by subjects, and what were the percentages of As and Bs and Cs. And all this was punctuated with in-jokes (usually disparaging) about the children.

The new staff were then issued with an astonishing document, which purported to explain the running of the school, parts of which I reproduce here in order to emphasize its real existence.

There is a set of school rules which are not called 'school rules' but 'General Information'. For example 'General Information no. 4' is 'Uniform regulations must be strictly observed'. No. 6 is 'Pupils must walk in single file on their right-hand side of the corridor at all times.' It is so silly, to my way of thinking. If we must have a uniform, why must we be strict about it? If the school does have a problem because of its ridiculous corridor why can we only bully the pupils into adopting a sensible rule-of-the-road for its use? Then in order to make the corridor more difficult to live with we have 'General Information no. 9'.

At the change of lessons, pupils will wait in the corridor outside their new rooms — orderly — until the teacher arrives. Pupils arriving after the rest of the class is seated will be deemed to be late.

My experience of the corridor so far is of a seething, wriggling mass of brown-clad bodies dotted at various levels from knee-high to well above my head by pink faces and toothy grins. At intervals along it the crowd parts and closes again round some respected disciplinarian like the cadaver of Welsh Mr Jones who loves to bawl, 'Get-into-the-right-what-do-you-think-you're-up-to?'

No. 16 states hopefully, 'Pupils will stand in single file in the bus queues. Any pushing or hooliganism will be severely punished.' I've never seen a single file bus queue after school and I've never seen any of the rapidly departing staff doing anything about it. But then nor have I seen anything that I could call hooliganism.

Although these rules are objectively trivial, it is very difficult to know, in a new situation, how one is expected to regard them. I would like to feel that I can be adult about this and take an independent line, but the rules seem to tell me to drop my independent judgement, and wear the accepted staff blinkers. So, instead of looking about me and interfering in pupil encounters when I think interference is justified and might achieve something, I have to inspect a piece of student conduct and say 'Does that constitute an infringement of "general information no. 16"?' The rules don't even allow me to think, 'Is that hooliganism?' I must think, 'Would Mr Jones, the discipline gog, call that "hooliganism"?'

This is all seriously disturbing. There is an assumption, which I've noticed pressing on me before, that 'discipline' (that special school word) is an external and objective entity which we teachers all agree about when we are not being tiresome. Thus, Mr Curle, the headmaster, said, in his inimitably involved way,

'Now, you new teachers, I know, some, I know you, some of you new teachers. We had a chap last year who had to leave because. What I'm saying is that DON'T be friendly with them to begin with; you must establish your DISCIPLINE first.'

And I nodded with the rest of them as though I understood what he meant. And then I found another echo of the idea in a crazy muddled document called, *The organization of forms 1–5.* Under the heading, 'General discipline', which of course I eagerly scrutinized, it says:

It is *generally* felt that the rules which exist at the moment, whether they be written down in black and white or are *commonly accepted by all members of the teaching profession*, are sufficient in themselves, but we would like to see all pupils observe them, and all staff to enforce them much more rigidly than at present.

When I look inside me for these 'commonly accepted rules' I find a shameful unpedagogical blank!

As far as the 'rigid' enforcement goes, and the 'severe punishment' the teacher's elbow is given strength by a pathetic little pantomime called the 'conduct competition'.

Roll up! Roll up, folks! See the incredible inter-house contest of conduct, work and games. See these little delinquents fighting to avoid the dreaded black marks which might smirch the honour of their house. See the little hooligans standing in single file at the bus stop – all done by the magic of black marks. Entrance to this exciting competition is not only absolutely free for all pupil members of Grove End School, it is actually compulsory. Roll up! Roll up!

We find the spirit of the thing set forth in *The organization of forms 1–5*.

Thus:

Conduct Competition
It was agreed that with conduct and general discipline we must work from a *standard of perfection* (sic!) and therefore marks can only be lost.

Sue and I are staying with friends while the more rotten parts of our crumbling new home are reinstated by the local builder, and we sit around in the evenings and laugh at this document with Tom and Alice, our hosts. Tom started teaching in a London comprehensive and is full of nightmare tales about the place. None of us has ever seen this teacherly self-righteousness set down so clearly in print. My laughter is rather hollow, because during the day I must surely be judged by the same standard of perfection, and just as surely my colleagues must find me wanting. And if I laugh whole-heartedly at them, am I just strapping on another armour-plating of conviction?

In the lower school I have four groups to teach, a First, a Second, a Third and a Fourth. First impressions are as follows:
1E. This is an unstreamed group of twenty-nine very diminutive and very polite and respectful people. Tim is a Biggles enthusiast, which surprised me, and Geoff has a father who teaches at the school.
2B. A huge group of quiet but so far very wary kids. Thirty-seven of them, and they don't do Latin or German. I teach them five lessons a week, each time in a different room, and in none of the rooms is there ever enough chairs for them all to sit down! We always start by breaking the spirit of 'General Information no. 12', when we disturb other classes in search of chairs and forgotten books and pens and so on.

3A. Another much smaller non-Latin-or-German group with a heavy male majority. This lot has shown me that they already have the blues. They already say 'poetry and all that rubbish', and 'we are the worst behaved group in the school, everyone tells us that'. Peter Langland stands out straight away by means of a consciously caricatured bumkin repartee full of 'bloody gerts' and 'Us casn't do that's'. This is surely offered as a challenge. 'Us and them' is already well developed here.

4E is the jet set. They will take the O-level in four terms from now. Marvellously quiet and attentive, with a large majority of girls – twenty-one to eight boys! In this situation the boys are understandably rather subdued.

3A: So far I have simply asked people to write on subjects of their own choice. I want to see how they react to that idea, and to see what they choose. Chris's piece, called *No Suitable Title*, gives an impression of well ordered industry about the lesson which was certainly not there in my perception of it.

No Suitable Title

We have been told to write an essay in our lesson. Nearly everyone has chosen a subject and are getting on well with it. My friend is writing about horses, another person is writing about comics, another about the history of Wembley, one about fishing and another about rugby. In fact there are only a few of us who do not know what to do. All around people are writing away at their chosen subject. There is laughter. The teacher is talking about fishing with a boy. By now my friend has almost written a page and I'm still wondering what I can write about. I'm wondering what to write because I have to hand in some work for the lesson. Could I write about fishing? No, someone is already writing about that. Aeroplanes? No, what do I know about them? I can as it is only just distinguish them now. Talking is developing among the class. Should I write about television? or, about my holiday? No, neither of those would be any good.

Already four have been handed in finished. Oh well, the bell's gone. One more period to go and then home. What a nice thought!

That sounds splendid. Just how I would like it to be, ordered, friendly even happy. In fact Peter Langland was clowning and causing fairly small eddies of chaos. He acts like a rustic goon and seems to expect me to accept him as one. The state of his English book, which is hardly used but is battered, coverless, torn and blotted, is a fair indication of his state of mind towards school.

But he did write.

'Can we *really* write anything we want to, sir?' he asked.

'Yes.'

'Really?' And he implies that I have asked for it, really asked for it.

'Yes,' I say, with rather less conviction.

'Cor!' and he leers and gives a sidelong glance and a libidinous giggle which infects that corner of the classroom. He decides to write about television.

'How do you spell "television"?' he asks, making it clear that this is not a real question.

'Tee,' I begin, and 'vee' I conclude.

He takes me at my word. 'TV' he writes for a title and he begins: 'The television is . . .' I leave him to it. But whenever he completes a line he tells me loudly across the room. Whenever he finishes a sentence he shows it to his pals. Their sniggers make my scalp twitch; I expect appalling obscenities and wonder how I will cope with the situation. But after all, here is the result.

The television is mainly shown at night time as many people
have come home from work by then. Many things are
shown on the television including puppets, cartoons,
science fiction, and modern-day happenings. The
Wednesday play is naughty. I know that because our
Muvver wont let me watch it. Our Dad likes watching the
Bluebell girls on the Ken Dodd show but our Muvver dont
like him doing it because you can see all their legs.
The Sierra Leone tribal dancers was good, our Dad said
he was only watching the women.

How much daring did it take to produce that?

2B's behaviour has declined rapidly. Perhaps I have been 'too friendly too soon'. To begin with they were quiet and wary, and they did as they were told. Three weeks later they do exactly as they want. There is one particularly depressing lesson last period on a Monday. They have a music test in the lesson before, forty minutes of rigorous silence. (I have seen their duplicated notes on the great composers ... 'Schubert's is the music of the happy man' ... and 'Haydn was the father of the string quartet'. I wonder what the test consists of? 'Is Schubert's music that of the happy man?') When they arrive at my lesson they are hopping like fleas.

Mr Daniels, the senior master, was standing just outside the door as the class whooped and cheered their way home after yesterday's lesson.

'Could I have a word with you, Mr Otty?'

'Certainly.'

We step into his room which, I notice with a chill, is directly across the corridor from my Monday 2B lesson.

'I'm sorry to have to mention this, but there seems to be rather a lot of noise coming from your second-year class. Would you like any help? I mean if I can give them a rocket or something ...'

Now, Mr Daniels is a nice man. A good man, I insist. He does use mild corporal punishment (the gym shoe) but with a cheerful conviction of its value and effectiveness. He is not a mean bully. Most important the children really like and trust him, even the ones he hits. He is an experienced and successful teacher.

From the front of my head I hear a distant, calm, reasonable voice. It tells Mr Daniels things I like to think, and it has no connection with the deep centred panic in my mind.

'That's very kind, Mr Daniels, but I would rather carry on on my own.'

'Oh well, that's fine, as long as you feel you have a grip on them when you need it.'

'No, I have no "grip on them", but then I don't want to have.' His eyebrows shoot up spreading wrinkles towards his bald crown. 'You see I don't want them to work for me because of *my* control. They must learn their own control, the value of cooper-ation and the intrinsic value of what they are studying ...'

Brave words, brave words. But he takes them – and he appears to be convinced.

The children seem incapable of encompassing my attitude towards homework. They really do not believe that I won't punish them for not doing it. Otherwise their reactions vary. The first form just get on with their work. They are not yet really involved in the school pastime of 'getting away with things'. The fourth form are given a theme each week which they can use if they want. Otherwise they can use their own ideas, and if they have no ideas they can do nothing. If this happens they are thrown into an agony of self-reproach. They desperately throw out excuses which save them from nothing. The second and third forms do nothing unless they have a really gripping idea. That seems all right to me until the authorities find out, but to 2B it seems immoral that I don't throw black marks about the place!

Peter Langland has done almost nothing since his television piece. (I was told that he expected a black mark for that.) His second effort was a so-called project on jokes. This was just a scruffy piece of paper with some mildly smutty stories on it. I didn't punish him for that either so he seems to have given up. He has also largely given up trying to disrupt the lessons, which is something gained.

But what about Nigel Moore? This is his second year in the third form. He did badly and 'caused trouble', I gather, so he has been kept back for a year. Now he is clearly neurotic. Even out of the classroom he can't talk *to* you. And I have to try to get him involved in work he has seen already, and I suspect he was bored by most of it last year. He already has six black marks, and I reckon if I used black marks as the other teachers do he would get six every time I saw him. But they make no difference. They produce no change in his real attitude to his situation, he just sees them as a constant part of what he has to put up with. I reckon he needs more sympathy than punishment. Keeping him back a year isolates him so disastrously – and by that tender criterion, his age. He is really raw about that. I mentioned the other day in the corridor that he was a bit older than the rest of the class and he was immediately in a funk. His eyes seemed to revolve like catherine wheels. Whatever we were discussing was lost in emphatic headshaking which made me quite dizzy.

'Me sir? No sir. Not really, sir, only a couple of months, sir, that's all, sir . . .'

Anyway I am determined not to resort to this punishment system which I deplore so strongly. I am sure I will soon be in an invidious position as far as the other staff are concerned, but I'll work that one out when we come to it.

The kids say, 'That's Mr Otty, he doesn't believe in homework.' ... 'He doesn't give black marks.' I think of the official line on discipline: 'Since we are aiming at a standard of perfection it was felt that marks could only be lost.' Sententious pigheaded, thick-thought crap! And I also think of those fourthform English exercise books. They are, perhaps, two thirds used. On the outside in the section headed 'class' it says '~~1E~~, '~~2E~~, '~~3E~~, '4E. And that is presumably with the statutory three written homeworks every week. But before I am found out I must be prepared with really good arguments.

Two contrasting pieces from the fourth form:

Night

Darkness engulfs the light
Everything is grey – black and now even blacker,
The last of the day has slipped away, night reigns,
A deathly hush arises, nothing stirs.
Darkness is cold, a stranger to one's feelings.
It hides the beauty of the world,
The beauty that is seen in daytime.
Darkness is frightening,
Noises become louder, loneliness stronger.
Two hours of light is one hour of darkness.
But night passes silently as most people sleep.
Now the crack on the ceiling appears,
Now the jumper on the floor can be seen,
At last the night yields to the day.
   People begin to move.
Once again the time of peace is over
   In front is another new day.

by Sally

That is fine. She's never read *Spelt from Sybil's Leaves*, and I don't think she would get much from it just yet. But I have, and my reaction to her poem is on safe ground therefore. But Joyce gave me a book of her poems, which are serious, and hers, written for herself, and I find them embarrassing and don't really know what to say to her.

The Apprentice

Let me in,
O Neptune,
Let me in, O King,
Into your wordless kingdom
Let this earthling in.

I want none of your jewels,
My eyes can give me these,
I only want freedom
To comb your tangled mass.
Give me nothing more
Just open up your door.

I have given my life
To pledge myself to you.
I love your sea-anemones,
I love your coral caves.
Here in Neptune's kingdom
I delve into your age.

There were several more with the same kind of group of images in them. The sea – the deep – the whirlpool-sinking. Octopus – anemone. Caverns. And an initiation idea. One can't just say to her 'these are bad', because, although they are filtered through poor second-hand notions of what poetry is, they nevertheless come from deep inside her. The (unconscious) love-initiation idea becomes clearer several attempts later in

The Whirlpool

It was clear and inviting,
Deep and exciting,
Moving and thrilling,
Carefree and willing,
Strangely enticing,
Maybe sufficing.

My mouth kept on thirsting,
My lungs nearly bursting,
My heart wildly thumping,
My knees freely bumping,
On the edge, I am thinking,
In the whirlpool I'm sinking.

From my tentative oblique inquiries I gather she has no idea what they are about. They just happen.

3A greeted me yesterday morning with a demand that they should have a debate.

'Right,' says I, 'what shall we have a debate about?'

'Sex-before-marriage!' a chorus of cries and the challenge stare from several quarters, Peter and Nigel particularly.

'How,' says the stare, 'does he get out of that one?'

'Right,' I can only answer, 'who wants to be the main speaker for it? Main speaker against? . . .' and so on.

And they really tried to make it work. They would not cooperate to begin with. They fooled about. They interrupted the speakers, missing half of what they had to say and throwing away their own ideas and arguments to their next neighbour who was anyway listening to someone else. And so they themselves had to organize themselves, impose their own silence so that they could hear each other's voices and ideas. And, really, I need not have worried about the occasion degenerating into an orgy of obscenity. They were so restrained and responsible – especially Nigel Moore whose ideas on sexual morality would grace a Sunday-school teacher, while the language in which he expresses them would disgrace a bargee. Peter kept very aloof, occasionally throwing in some appallingly crude remark about 'scrubbers' or 'virgins'.

But when I arrived for today's lesson, Jones the discipline had got hold of them. In direct contravention of 'General Information no. 9' I allow 3A to go into their classroom at the beginning of a lesson instead of cluttering up the corridor, and tripping and punching the other pupils who have to pass them. But Jones had bawled them out. As I arrived they were standing in two lines against the wall looking sulky and resentful.

'NOW-IN-YOU-GO-GIRLS-FIRST-WHO-DO-YOU-
THINK-YOU-ARE-STOP-PUSHING-MOORE-RICHARDS-
JOHNSON-BURNHAM-SHUT-UP-WHEN-I'M-TALKING-
STAND-UP-STRAIGHT-LINE-UP-THOSE-DESKS.'

Then he comes over smiling patronizingly at me standing feeling feeble and cross in the doorway. Quietly pitying my incompetence he says, 'I'll just have another shout at them, if you don't mind, Mr Otty,' in the softest Welsh confidential murmur.

'Er ... ahem,' I respond, boldly, but already the old hand is deep in his raucous demonstration.

'DON'T-MOVE-THE-DESKS-THE-PRIVILEGES-YOU-
PEOPLE-TAKE-FOR-YOURSELVES-I-DON'T-KNOW-HOW-
CAN-A-BUNCH-OF-HOOLIGANS-LIKE-YOU-EXPECT-
WHAT'S-SO-FUNNY-BIGGS?-JONES?-I'LL-MAKE-YOU
LAUGH-ON-THE-OTHER-SIDE-OF-AND-YOU-FELLS!'

There is a silent atmosphere of mutiny. Exit the old sweat smiling at the success of his demonstration because the atmosphere if mutinous, is, after all, silent. The closing door behind his back releases a mutter of 'silly old basket', and 'stupid old sod', and the lesson did not go well.

I was talking about that last incident with Tom last night, and he told me a story, from his London comprehensive days, which made me think.

There was this bloke there who was what Tom calls a 'gwg'. ('Gwg' is a word from Tom's Welsh youth. It is a nonsense syllable, pronounced somewhere between gog and goog, which he uses to abuse certain kinds of ranting narrow pedagogues.) Anyway, this man was a real disciplinarian, and much admired in that difficult jungle school. He was particularly proud of being able to walk into the hall, the playground, the classrooms, and to produce a magical silence simply by his silent presence. He used to describe in the staff-room, how on their summer camping holidays, he would make his own children square off their kit in military fashion every morning, and stand by their sleeping-bags while he inspected it.

He taught maths, and, Tom says, in a school where 'most teachers only managed to mark their registers on a good day', he was able to get the pupils to do some real work. When someone was trying to start an adventure playground in the area, he was dead against the idea; according to him, 'if you give 'em a pigsty you'll make pigs of 'em'.

But having said all that, Tom's main point about him was that he was hell to follow. If you had a class the lesson after he'd had them, they were surly, rebellious, impossible.

2B. Lynn writes on *Friends.*

Having friends is good and without them you would be very lonely. It makes me feel very sad when I think of poor elderly people living on their own.

When you're thirteen you've got a lot of friends, but as you get older they move and you're lonely. You run to your parents, but they grow old and wish to be alone.

Making friends is part of growing up and being shy presents problems. So the best thing to do is pal up with another shy person. If you are too forward then many times people dislike you.

Two days ago she wrote this:

I will not do any work and you cannot make me. Teachers think they can tell us to do anything and we'll do it but I won't. I am myself and I don't care what people think about me. So there.

At school it's all do this do that. Why should I write just to pass some stupid exams. Everything we do is BORING and STUPID. I think a teacher should be able to control a class without using black marks and detentions. But you won't control me.

Which is the real Lynn? I usually see her with her head laid back, eyes narrowed, mouth wide full of pirhana teeth, shouting hatred and rebellion, and her 'shy' pal joins in with a vivid will. They say (the psychologists) that Lynn's kind of behaviour is often a cover for insecurity. ... But I don't know what to do in the midst of thirty-seven screamingly insecure second formers.

A bleak November Saturday in the dim middle of this interminable term, and instead of recreating myself I am volunteered by unspoken blackmail to take two rugby teams to an away match. The rain has fallen steadily now for twenty-four hours. As I drive to school the fields on either side of the road have standing water on them. I am sure the matches will be cancelled. But no, the pitches are in fine shape, we are told, so off we go. On the coach the boys manifest traditional behaviour. Tunelessly they shout filthy songs, and hoarsely they bellow sporting war-cries into which the name of the school can be slotted. 'Bow-wow! Moo! Baa! Quack-quack! grunt! GROVE END!' I huddle, ill-natured against a streaming window and read a book.

At the pitch I am greeted by pink and jovial sports-masters who grip my hand to demonstrate their physical fitness.

'Bit wet,' they say, their words mixing hot steam with the cold rain, 'Still, be all right once we get going.'

Outside the smelly little pavilion the sky has moved closer. The rain falls with an unspectacular but impressive persistence. The hut is surrounded with a shallow and irregular moat of muddy water. Soon the boys neat and brisk in rugger kit leap the moat and trot through the gloom to the distant pitches. The pink and jovial sports-masters are now displaying white and knobbly knees. They say they must be mad, but they don't believe it; they are happy.

Some atavistic guilt makes me feel that I too ought to be stand-ing out there in the mud, soaking up the rain and cheering on the school. Instead I retire to the smelly little hut and chat with the groundsman. He watches the knobbly knees of the sports-masters twinkling through the rain.

'They must be mad,' he says, and he does mean it. He turns from the steamy window, and from his pitches being churned to quagmires and he brews us a cup of tea.

On the way back (both teams having thoroughly lost) there are more filthy songs and more shouts. And there is the mild mob violence that goes with these occasions. Collins is debagged. I don't notice what is happening until it has happened, and in any case in my present mood, I don't want to do anything about it. (Black marks can hardly be suitable on a rugger outing, can they?) I hardly know any names anyway.

The laughter as I stand uncertainly up and try to rescue Collins, is harsh, unpleasant, challenging. I see the same blank challenge on every face but Collins's which is twisted with pain as he sits humiliated on the floor of the coach in his underpants and nurses a trodden hand.

'Give him back his clothes.'

'I haven't got them, sir.'

'I don't know where they are.'

The same laughter from each of them, the same mask of idiocy, the same glances shared. To refuse communication is the strongest weapon of the group. They act like a single many-headed half-wit. Gradually the clothes are assembled. Collins is decent once more, missing only a shoe.

'You all right?' I ask.

'Yes, sir,' cheerful now the necessary ordeal is over, the group appeased. He's bloody well got to be cheerful with all those frozen grimaces of group cheerfulness surrounding him. He's got to be on their side, one of the group, or the group will use him again to demonstrate the unity of the group. The power of group weapons! But why must they be weapons? And why do they need this iron group which inhibits them individually with a harsher and nastier discipline than any that the school imposes?

For the first time since coming to Grove End I really dislike some children. I recall a squad of regular soldiers in the next barrack-room beating up one of their own number because they were hard men, and group-drunk and a squad . . . and the fear and hatred that ran through me when the infantry men thrashed and clubbed so called 'suspects' in revenge for a murder in Nicosia . . . and the animal identities of the boat crews at Cambridge, throwing bottles, fighting to burn their boats on the bonfires after the bump-supper and shouting and pissing and eventually vomiting their triumphant groupness all over the college.

Back at the school I am given three mocking, hoarse, group cheers for what they see as my leniency. And the boys depart their several ways, and regain, thank God, their individual identities.

I feel fantastically isolated here, in the Grove End staff common room. It is not that it is a formal staff, or that they are unkind to me. It may, indeed, all be inside my head – I imagine they must be saying that Otty is 'having trouble'. I imagine some of them agreeing that I make their life more difficult by not giving black marks and by not setting homework. As I pace uneasily at the extreme edge of the three circles, adding my cigarette smoke to the blue fug, I just think that I don't want to be school-masterly like them. It is amazing how many of them wear muted, mouldy-green clothes, corpse green, camouflage green, the greens of nature in retreat, in decay. And all too often we just don't talk the same language. Ernest Hopkins can get in a moral rage about things which only cause a slightly quickened interest in me. His face crimsons, his joints shake, and his up-reared bushy eyebrows seem to wriggle in protest! What gets me most, I suppose, is that they seem generally to be content with the school as it is. Apart from Hugh Evans (spherical and architypally Welsh) they have no deep concern about improving education – and he is new, like me, so he doesn't count for much.

I suppose that's why I have to communicate with this diary. I started because in the end I found I enjoyed doing it on teaching practice and because it threw my experience into a helpful kind of relief. Now I need to carry on to grind things out of my system!

Another piece from Peter Langland

My Enemies

My Enemies are all teachers and coppers and parents and all people with authority. The worst few teachers I hate are Jeremiah (Jenkins), Ethel (Graham) that short top-heavy fat thing, head-slapper or 'laddie' Jones, Ernest Hopkins, the one with the bloody gert eye-brows and just because he knows all about music he thinks we should. He's a bastard.

I hate all coppers 'cause they all come round our house when anything happens 'cause I do everything.

Up our other school, Fanny Black she used to make me sit on a little stool about six inches above the ground. Just 'cause I kept cheeking her.

I hate to think what Ernest Hopkins's eyebrows would do if he read that! And I can't do justice to the contempt written into the illustration and into the whole layout of the piece.

But if that was depressing, this piece, by Dick Clarke (also 3A), was not.

Autumn

As the biting wind blows, it grips the sentenced leaves from
the dark trees. They flutter down, unconcerned. Red,
yellow, golden; battered by the weather. As the wind blows
another gust they speed, with fluttering colour, along the
deserted grass. They come to rest, but quickly they begin to
whirl round as if chasing each other. Only the park-keeper
is left now, still sweeping up after the frustrating summer.
He begins to sweep up the leaves into neat piles on the
path. He finishes and turns from the wind to light a
cigarette. While his back is turned these leaves start up
again on their never-ending journey to nowhere.
Unhappily, the park-keeper (near retirement) begins again,
swearing to himself.

It was accompanied by a lovely sensitive double-page drawing.

This is a tremendous boost to me. His last effort (infected by
Peter and Nigel) was an ambitious piece of phoniness about a
police raid on a warehouse which had been converted into a
gigantic brothel!

Conversation with head of the English Department . . .

'Oh, Nick.'

'Yes.'

'I thought I'd better tell you that Mr Curle has mentioned to
me that your classes are rather noisy.'

'Oh.'

'It's all right. I shouldn't worry. He thinks you're doing all
right, he's not worried. He specifically mentioned that he was
sure you have no discipline problems. It's just that he has said
that your lessons are rather noisy, and I thought I ought to let
you know what he said.'

'Hm.'

'He also asked me to talk to you about setting homework . . .'

'How does he know about that?'

'Asks the kids, I shouldn't wonder.'

'Oh.'

'Look, Nick, you do what you think is right. Curle just asked
me to mention it to you, so I have. All right?'

'Yes.'

So it was not a passing cloud or a bit of dry rot that I saw floating outside the corridor window ... it was Curle on the prowl. What on earth made him conclude that I had no discipline problems?

Peter Langland's last piece on his enemies, was followed by an entirely voluntary offering! He called it a project, and it was on the *Marie Celeste*. It was not very good, much of it copied or rewritten from a source book. But it *was* eight sides long, and it *was* bound quite neatly with blue string, and it *did* have a picture of a contorted, neurotic-looking galleon on the front cover. Most important of all (when you consider the homework controversy) he had done it unasked, in his own time, and he had been interested and stirred by the story.

At last he was being, not natural, but boyish. He was interested and excited by something appropriate to his age. I had the curious sensation that he was shedding years as I talked with him. He was not, as usual, guarded, challenging my authority, swaggering, swearing, always keeping an eye out for sex. I got a jolt to see what he could be like but for his reaction to adults.

I gather he is savagely fond of animals, and very good with them. I say 'savagely' because, according to his friend Alan, he will brutally bully any kid he finds maltreating an animal. What a puzzle! Have I mentioned that he and Nigel Moore are famous? In the staff room, when teachers are groping for examples of nightmare pupils, their names seem to leap to mind.

Discussion over lunch with Bill Spinks and John Henderson.

Someone mentioned at lunch that the Plowden report had recommended the abolition of corporal punishment in primary schools, and had quoted a very high figure for the percentage of teachers who used it.

'Good thing too,' said John Henderson, which, since it was ambiguous, led to the question, 'Which bit was good? Abolition or use?'

'A bit of physical force did no one any harm,' he went on. 'When other methods fail, then the cane, or a tap however light it may be, is the answer.'

This led to my first real discussion about education with

anyone at Grove End Grammar School. John, who is a stern but straight fellow, with a sense of humour and a real warm concern for the children, nearly aborted the conversation by taking the 'when – you've – had – a – family – as – long – as – I – have – m' lad' line, and the 'as - a - very - much - married - man - with – three – children – who – has – always – been – inclined – to – spare – the – rod – I – can – see – now – that – it – would – have – been – better – if – I – had – used – it – on – occasion' gambit.

I protested that this was an unfair argument. It was not what we were talking about. First, that was the home not the school. Second, if accepted, it would simply mean that if we did not think like John by the time we were his age, we would be wrong. (That sounds to me like one of the grounds of the grammar-school mind, actually.) Callow though this was, it meant that the discussion continued. Spinks and Henderson *v.* Otty. I shall attempt a summary; since I am still smarting it will no doubt be biased.

John said he would use violence (sorry, he never used that word) corporal punishment in his family in order to produce ways of behaving in his children which he believed to be right. He agreed that if you believed it was right not to impose your views on others by means of violence, then violence would be an odd way of imposing this particular view. 'You bloody well accept that it is wrong to belt people until they accept what you say, or I'll belt you!'

He also brought up those wretched exempla Langland and Moore. They deserved the cane, he said, they would benefit from it. (Moore was regularly given the gym-shoe last year – he is still a problem this year.) After all other methods – by which he means all other punishments, i.e. black marks and detentions – have failed, then the cane is the only answer.

'When the cane fails,' I asked, 'what then? Why not kick the offender? Thumbscrews, maybe? Imprisonment?' This was ignored with a grimace because it had gone too far. We must be reasonable. That is we must not take reason too far.

So I tried another quite different tack. I said that what school crimes amounted to, more often than not, were instances of rudeness. See them listed in the black-mark book, 'talking', 'incessant talking', 'impudence', 'disobedience'. For example, a teacher is

told by an angry thirteen-year-old, that he is a stupid old git.
(This was not far-fetched. A fortnight ago a teacher told Nigel
Moore that he was so stupid she could not imagine how he got
into the grammar school. He replied, in kind, 'and I can't imagine how you ever got a job here you stupid old crud'. Nigel was
in trouble, not the teacher.)

At this point Bill Spinks took over.

'Now that's something I really will not take. If a boy said that
kind of thing to me, I'd take a really strong line and show him
what's what.'

But it doesn't worry me if the kids don't treat me like a time-
bomb! Apart from a momentary shock it does not insult me
deeply if an angry boy or girl (or adult) calls me ... what? A
fool? an ass? a crud? tight? According to Spinks I must therefore
have a thicker skin than he has. But whatever my resistance to
insult, I have enough sensitivity to know that to accuse him of
hypersensitivity on matters touching his dignity, arising from a
fundamental lack of confidence, would be as much of an affront
to him, as his accusation of insensitivity was to me. So, or
perhaps but, I made no accusation, and the discussion ended.

My fourth form almost always ignore my suggestions for writing. But they almost always write. Every Monday two-thirds of
them, at least, hand in their books, and marking them is not a
chore. I never know what I will find in them. Look at these two:

Time and Tide

There are gulls whistling and crying overhead. The sky is
grey and dark, the darkness broken only by a great hot
orange shield which is the sun.

Tiny waves wash onto the beach, recede then come
again, eating the black sand away beneath my feet. How
many more high tides will there be? How many more times
will the gulls build their nests?

It is getting colder now, the seasons are coming round
faster. Day-time, night-time all a meaningless jumble.
Always there is the orange disc in the sky, but, is it my
imagination? Is it getting smaller? More like a bowl than a
shield now.

The waves are bigger, towering and powerful. The sand is changing colour, new plants seem to be growing. The gulls have gone but in their place are curious new creatures. The crabs are changing becoming bigger, taller, scalier.

The climate is changing again, hotter and more humid. Eclipse follows eclipse. There are new stars in the night sky.

The crabs are even bigger now, growing and growing until they are thirty feet high, with long thin necks and heavy bodies. The beach is becoming swampy, wet, with tall trees emerging. The air is hot, clammy, and the night is filled with the bellows of two great animals fighting.

The bowl is now a plate. Colder, hotter, colder again. Very cold with ice creeping slowly over the swamps. No creatures now, only a few soft jelly fish in the water, but soon they will be frozen solid. A huge deluge of acid rain, melting the ice, filling the seas further.

Monstrous waves, bigger than before, crashing onto the shore. Earthquakes pushing up mountain ranges, to volcanoes showing hot circles of molten lava.

The disc is tiny now, like a saucer a long way away, nearly always in eclipse. The sky is nearly black, with a few tinges of purple.

Hotter now, despite the sun. More volcanoes. No land, no sea, nothing but volcanoes. Fire. The earth is melting bursting into flame.

The sky is invisible through the haze and smoke, but the sun has disappeared.

The light has been turned off. The sands of time have run out.

by Susan

She drew a line under the end of the piece and then wrote 'I'm sorry to have written such meaningless rubbish, but I'm so mixed up that everything I sit down to write comes out differently and I can't express what I want to.'

The piece seems remarkable to me, and very strange. It is not just science fiction of the mix-it-up-and-make-it-nice variety; there is too much feeling behind it for that. But if she didn't know what she was doing, how did she do it?

Fiona, on the other hand, writes brilliantly controlled stuff.

She has no worries about not being able to express what she wants to. She simply writes, and then waits to see if I will understand it.

Through Misted Glass

The heat of breath in the room,
Of sweating bodies and untranslated speech
Has misted up the window.

I wish I were outside
With the planet called world, and life,
That does not say that I should work
And not live my own life.

But they have misted up the glass,
Because of the two world's contrast,
And when I go outside they come too,
And I look inside then to warmth and peace,
But I am even further away from
What I love,
Because the glass is misted up
From the other side.

In the English course book I find this kind of suggestion for work:
    'Make a box analysis of the following sentences:
1. Ringing the wrong Smiths wastes time and temper.'
Or this:
    Prepared dictation:
1. The Privy Council won't accept pencil.
4. They will leave their heirs their heirlooms.'
Or this:
    'Revision Test:
Write a story consisting of three paragraphs properly planned and properly linked.'
    Talk about the tail wagging the dog. It is just the stuff to reach for when you remember at the last minute that the rules insist on a written homework tonight.
    So I've been using my copy of *Reflections* with 3A, and it really does work. They started by showing an interest in crime. I read them a bit from *The courage of his convictions*. Then two

bits from *Borstal Boy*, his arrival at the first prison, and his arrival at the borstal. They simply wanted to hear more (particularly the hard nuts), so I read a couple of bits from Frank Norman's *Bang to Rights*, and the extract from *Borstal Boy* in *Reflections*.

There was some good discussion, and one good piece of writing, but I really learnt something about Grove End, in those few lessons. The catchment area is not really a tough one. It is just a mean and accidental suburban sprawl of two-storey Victorian terraces, with a variety of non-conformist chapels, and a sprinkling of drab little shops. It is slashed by a couple of main roads with lorries and buses grinding in and out of the centre of the city. It has a narrowly respectable non-conformist atmosphere about it. But beneath what Allerton and Parker call 'the terrifying dreariness' of the lives of people who go 'straight', there is the world of Peter Langland and Nigel Moore, on the edge of which are John and Alan and Philip, which borders all the time on delinquency. There are fights 'up the youth clubs', and window smashings and petty thefts. I wonder how aware the other teachers are of this.

But now I have been 'on the carpet'. Summoned to the headmaster's study I find both Mr Curle and Miss Prynne looking grave. Miss Prynne is pursing her lips and puffing through them, as though she is about to blow a valve. I am transported back in time to naughty boy occasions from my schooldays. A strong connecting link is the wish I have now, and always had then, that I knew which of my many crimes has been detected. Black marks? – Homework? – Discipline in 2B? In fact it is a total surprise. Emotion seems to have blasted Mr Curle's syntax, so it is with difficulty that I sort out the story. Some parent in an anonymous phone call to Miss Prynne has accused me of recommending all my third-year pupils to have sexual intercourse before the age of twenty-one.

I stoutly deny the charge, but admit to having held a discussion with 3A about sex before marriage. Miss Prynne gulps with amazement and then puffs on. She remains silent, however, and leaves me shadow boxing with the strange shattered brilliance of Mr Curle's mind.

'It's too early in your, you, perhaps you lack the, it needs experience to tackle such a subject.'

'I didn't tackle it exactly. They brought it up and wanted to talk about it.'

'Well, subjects, I think it would be, subjects like this really come under my "Education for Adult Life" course.' (Two lessons in the first year to show them that rabbits do it; two lessons in the fourth year to hint that some married, Christian, adult humans do it too; two lessons in the sixth year for any questions.)

'But they wanted to talk about it *now*, not the January after next. I do feel it is important, Mr Curle, to take these matters as they arise naturally for the children.'

'Oh, I quite agree, but it takes a lot of know-how to guide a discussion of that kind.'

'A guided discussion is not a discussion. I can't decide their conclusions before we start.'

'Of course, of course, I'm with you all the way there, but sooner, or, sometime, sooner or later they, they will turn round and ask you what you think about it.'

'They did.' (Double gulp from Prynne.)

'And what did you do?'

'I told them. What else can one do?'

Always he came about at the last second, just when I thought we were all going to capsize under a blast of mindless authority, and he would declare that he agreed entirely, or he would certainly not advocate dishonesty. School teachers are, after all, committed to reason, however irrational are the postures they frequently adopt.

I had not made the recommendation, so I could not ask 'so what?' After all, it could have been a sound moral injunction, and it would still, in that case, remain sound even if Mr Curle and all the anonymous parents disagreed with it. Are people to be disbarred from teaching because of their views on sex; or are they to be disbarred from discussing sex unless they have had their views approved by Mr Curle? Then again teachers must know that their pupils ignore most of the advice they are given. Think of reports. 'She should work harder' . . . 'He should apply himself more.' . . . No one really expects the pupil to take that to heart and act on it, even if no one wants to admit it. Why should a suggestion like 'You should all have sex before you are twenty-one', be any more effective? It all assumes that what is good is dull and what is attractive is wicked. What if I had suggested that they should commit murder before they reached twenty-one? I suspect that no one would have reported me to the head for that, because the morality of murder is not so ambiguous. It is only because sexual morality is disputed territory (and therefore of great interest to young people, and also therefore a subject that needs a great deal of honest discussion) that anyone suggests that it ought not to be frankly discussed.

Back in the classroom with 3A and their real moral dilemmas, here's a piece by Peter Langland. For once it contains no challenge to my teaching authority, though it is certainly concerned with authority.

A Person I Know

This certain person is obviously barmy. If he saw an ornament on a doorstep (a little gnome or something like it) he'd pinch it just for the fun of it. It started off at a certain butcher's shop in our area. It was very easy to open the window at the back and pinch the money from the till. This certain boy broke in every Sunday afternoon until he was caught. He was too young to go to court, but he grassed on four other boys including his brother and the other three I knew particularly well. The three I know had CDs (conditional discharges) and the other two years probation. This still did not stop him. His mates and him stole 8,000 fags from a pub and there is still 3,000 not recovered.

His criminal career carried on, breaking into shops, houses, Embassy gift-show vans, and finally Brown's at Newtown. He was caught leaving the premises with £350 and his mates had a bike, fishing rods, fishing tackle valued at about £150. He was put away for five years and he has escaped seven times in the three months he has served so far.

With this kind of experience in his mind, it is not really to be wondered at that he regards black marks for cheek as petty. Is it all right to discuss it with him? Would Curle and Prynne mind?

I told Tom last night about my encounter with Mr Curle over the alleged sex-before-marriage incident. As always he had a tale to tell which brought a curious kind of comfort.

In his early days at his London school, when he was getting really fed up with the apparently unstoppable chaos of some of his lessons, he decided to go and see his headmaster about it. He remembered that this was the official advice offered at his training college – as he said, he had noted it down in his lecture notes and had duly regurgitated it in his exams – 'When having persistent discipline problems go and discuss the matter frankly with your headmaster, and seek his advice.' On the face of it, it does seem a sensible thing to do.

Tom said that the head was clearly rather embarrassed, but made various platitudinous suggestions like 'sort out the rogues and make them sit at the front', or 'get them to put their hands on their heads'. Idiotic suggestions, because, as Tom said, if you could get them to do *that* you did not have discipline problems.

But the point of the story was this. The head apparently got hold of a teacher who was known to be friendly with Tom. Via this third person he intimated to Tom that it was rather unprofessional to seek HM's advice over discipline difficulties. The friend himself was utterly amazed at what he saw as Tom's near criminal lunacy. 'What do you want to go and tell the old man about that for?'

As long as your problems don't actually spill beyond the classroom, then all can be said, officially, to be well – and that is all that matters.

I do not like being an *enfant terrible*. It invokes the positional passions, the emotions generated by differences of status, and these prevent clear talk about the matter in hand. God knows, I am uncertain enough about the central issues of teaching – I can't also fight a rearguard action on all those trivial irritations such as form positions, totting up and balancing my register, reports, homework (which looms ugly once again). And yet it is because people have no time and energy to argue about form positions that the farce continues with no one believing in it.

Mr Curle asked me today if I had had this book (*Reflections*) vetted by my head of department. That is positional talk – don't discuss the book, relate it to the hierarchy.

But the second form are back at their very worst. And now I have stupidly and inconsistently half-committed myself to using black marks next lesson. The thing is that I cannot use them without assuming a mask of angry hostility which I regard as the last failure of a teacher or of a human being. And another thing is that I was panicked into this situation by seeing the headmaster looming greyly through the corridor window.

Sylvia Ashton-Warner mentions the knees of guilt pressing on the throat; a really excellent description of what it feels like as I carry my shameful incompetence pick-a-back with me.

I'm not the only one who's cheesed off with the dump. Here is my fourth-form Susan in an unsolicited piece about:

School
Grey skies and racing clouds. Stark bare trees silhouetted against the buildings. Miserable and ugly. Prison.
School.
  Nearly Christmas but no goodwill.
  Cold. Form periods. Boredom. Noughts and crosses on torn-up rough-books.
  Latin test, French test, History. Reports, School play, a touch of light and colour. Then the carol service. Squeaky flat singing.
  More tests. A never ending jumble. Crowded corridors a swarming mass of brown. Pencil sharpenings on the floor. Ink. Paper. Notes.
  Another test. Wellington. Waterloo 1814? The river has waterfalls in its upper course. Participles, verbs, adverbs.
  Dirty window panes, chalk dust, scruffy classrooms.
  Rows of silent bicycles in an equally silent shed. Mustn't talk in form rooms, mustn't eat, must wash. Black marks, detentions, regulations, homework.
  Hockey match. Mud. Bruised legs. Cold. Shrieking girls. Encouraging. Enthusiastic. Over what?
  Crates of empty milk bottles, soggy stinking straws. Assembly in the mornings, pray, sing, but don't talk. Head

master preaching, no one listens. Deals out punishment.
More black marks. Teachers leaving. Swearing scandals.
Dinner times. Muck. Custard in the water. Gravy on the
tables
    Clothes checks. Kit checks. Just like the army.
    What would happen if we all walked out?

Well, the term is over. The head's control of his native
language became more and more tenuous. At the final assembly
he addressed the school for forty-five minutes about 1 Cor-
inthians, 13. 'Though I speak with the tongues of men and of
angels and have not love, I am become as sounding brass or a
tinkling cymbal.' I don't know what kind of divided tongue he
was speaking with, but subordinate clauses and parentheses
sprouted and branched from incomplete subordinate clauses
until the head spun with the wasted effort of attempting to recol-
lect where he began. And just as one had it pinned down, some
startling and random recollection, about meteorology, or when I
was your age, was thrown up by the fruit machine of his mind,
and set everything at odds again. I thought the children were
wonderful to tolerate it, but at length he wound himself down at
the far end of a blind alley of total irrelevance. Inadvisedly he
attempted to get going again by means of what was supposed to
be a rhetorical question.
    'Well, where do we go from there?'
    There were several impatient shouts of 'Home', and 'on hol-
iday', and Mr Curle immediately became so 'wroth' that 'he was
out of alle charitee'.
    So, forgetting St Paul, he berated us all for our misplaced
sense of humour. Then we sang 'Jerusalem' and 'God save the
Queen', and in solemn silence he declared the term closed.
    In the December dusk I walked along the tow-path between
the canal and the estuary under a flat grey sky and through a
steely drizzle. Everything in sight was long and flat and black or
grey. The mud, the canal, the sea, the sunken channel of the low-
tide river, all cold and horizontal. A derelict railway bridge
stretched, span by span, long and broken, across sand, mud,
water, mud, sand again. And near at hand derelict barges rotted
coldly, and settled, deeper and more heavily in the grey mud.

Spring term

It is even worse after the holiday. I had not believed, I discover, that the folly of 'Jerusalem' and 'God save the Queen' could really persist. I was sure it must be all in my jaundiced mind, not out there in the real world. The fool of a lab technician had failed to record the first of the term's broadcasts (which seriously reduces the point of the rest of them). The second-form group are as bad as their worst times last term. The third form, after a considerable improvement, are worse now, I think, than ever before. And for a week I had a black oily acid chewing at my solar plexus. I was determined to leave teaching. I would take up the law, become a barrister, anything. I would go barefoot and stubbly and think, I would. . . .

But then some of the second form recorded part of a play and they learnt so much from it they were overwhelmed, and gained enormous impetus for more writing. And Fiona in the fourth form, after being introduced to Cummings and Hopkins (punctuation and grammar!) wrote this splendid and remarkable poem:

Mistlethrush

O your cold notes
thistleringly piercing
they bring perhaps tears to
my maybe eyes,
but not really i have
heard it all before
This moon-in-june stuff
i don't care if the moon is full
or the grass is green
or there is dew on the rose
or the stars in your deep pools-of-molten-beauty
shallow eyes . . .

but i do really
and what matters to me is
that there are some
people
(show me, don't say they are everyplace)
(have you looked? have you eyes?)
who are deep and lonely
and hungry beautiful
with minds that their bodies fit O
cleanly and silently
hardly there
and then (maybe don't say, really i tell you)
i am not ashamed to cry.

And a bird singing in the snow
is only a bird singing in the snow
but i don't think so
and it doesn't matter
(believe me)
if you do.

I find it difficult to believe that a fourth former could really write like that. I get in a panic (suspecting an ambush behind everything) and imagine she has copied it out to test me. I think it is too sophisticated, too adult; but it is by her.

In spite of (and partly because of) the deterioration of 3A, I have had a curious exchange with Alan Johnson. He has normally sat moody and silent and blessedly still through even my worst lessons. The staff regard him as low-grade material. At the end of last term, he suddenly wrote a piece about 3A. It was mainly crude abuse of the rougher elements, but it also complained about my being 'too soft' with them. When I gave it back to him with some comment about it not being very fair on his mates, or on me, he said:

'All right. I wrote a piece about the form. Now you do it. You try.'

I could only agree to try. And, during the holidays, I did try, and every time I wrote a word I thought of the potential repercussions. I could not mention any individuals when he was going to read it. So I gave up. Perhaps, I thought hopefully, he will have forgotten.

But no. At the beginning of this term, up he comes during our first lesson.

'Have you written that essay yet?'

'Well, I began it. It's very difficult, you see I can't mention any names – that wouldn't do – I'll have to try again.'

'O.K.'

After another week up he comes again. In the tone of a patient schoolmaster cajoling for a piece of late homework.

'Do you think you could get it done by Monday, sir?'

'O.K.'

Mercifully I remembered, and this is what I wrote.

III A

They are full of life. Within the group there is more variety of individual behaviour and character than in any other group I teach at present. They also all have plenty of intelligence and, in a way, as individuals, they have responsibility. For example, I can't imagine being embarrassed at meeting one of them out of school. Person to person, outside the classroom, they are as pleasant and friendly as I could wish for. But what happens *in* the classroom?

Knowing that the class is composed of individuals like those I have described, I have refused to treat them collectively as though they were a bunch of sub-intelligent criminals past the reach of human communication. The reaction we all know. It will pass . . . a month, a year, a term, I don't know, but the logic of the situation must eventually prevail, and things will change.

In the meantime, if I can get some well written and well thought pieces from the class: if I can get some boys or girls to read something with genuine personal interest: if I have a good conversation with someone in the group then something is being achieved. And I think it is more worthwhile than an imposed routine of meaningless exercises.

If English is still, for many members of 3A, no more than a safety-valve – an opportunity for striking matches, swearing, giggling (noble pursuits) – then it is, after all, doing something, however small, for them. It must eventually do more, and it could be doing less.

Well it was in the end quite honest.

Alan took my essay, went to his desk and read it twice straight away. Then he came out to the front, grabbed a piece of paper, and sat down again to write his reply. For the rest of the lesson he was encased in an invisible capsule, impervious both to my attempts to teach, and 3A's mixed responses. Here is what he handed me at the end of the lesson:

Your point of view is very interesting. It shows to me the hardships of teaching. As to your question of what happens when a class comes together in one big group instead of several small groups, I think that I would be in the best position to answer, because I am with them in a group all day.

The main reason is, I think, that they show off, they want to be known by everybody and the only way people like Nigel Moore can be known is by being the stupid clown of the class. Langland is the bully, and Gordon Small is the big soft type on who all Langland's bullying is based. The three are known by most of the people in the school.

Why did they start bullying and stupidness? The answer is that in the first and second year Moore was all right, or so my next-door neighbour, who was in his class tells me. And then he wanted to get known and he was bored, so he neglected school work and found that people noticed him and so he became a proper dunce and now people know him.

Langland was bad at the primary. He just likes fighting and he has an uncanny knack of getting into trouble. These two combined got others thinking about being noticed, so now if Moore says 'I'm doing no homework' no one does any homework. Teachers think they're no good and bullies. But they are usually unhappy. They might be noticed but they are unhappy at the way they have got people to notice them, and they feel very unhappy.

They like some teachers and so they say hello in the corridor when none of the gang are there. But they're scared to do it in class because they know they will be called ponce, etc. and be chucked out of the gang and will have to start from the beginning and that scares them stiff.

That is very impressive, I think. He is fourteen and he writes with so much more thought, about how his peers work, than one finds in those staff-room clichés about 'sorting out the rogues and making them sit at the front', or about 'not being too friendly until you have established your discipline'. It is so much wiser. Look at the sympathy with which he can understand how the individual feels about his particular bargain among the group roles, and look how *he* knows that the group exerts pressures independently of what the individual desires. We staff always blame the individual and then punish him.

And that last bit surely lays bare the workings of punishment in the group logic. It is used by us teachers to reinforce, to stabilize, to maintain, the distribution of roles within the group. We say we use it to change conduct, but in fact it keeps it the same. The 'naughty boy's' identity within the group is marked by the punishment he earns, and he courts punishment for that reason. If you want to change him from a 'naughty boy' into something else, then clearly you have to stop punishing him. Of course, when you do, he will demand punishment more and more loudly as he feels his role slipping away from him. In some ways it is crueller than punishment but if you can stand it and can support him through it, it must surely lead to change (if that's what you want – and that's what teachers *say* they want).

One of my 2B lessons takes place next door to the head's study. The kids don't in the least appreciate what that means to me. The room is furnished with cast-iron seat-desks, or desk-seats. A kind of combination man-trap and sledge. There are only thirty-two of them in the room so at least five of them have to have two occupants. There's fine brawling potential for you. Why should I have to sort that one out?

This morning – my nerves are still twanging from the incident – one of the boys brought his pet stick insects to school. They were very impressive, a vivid green and much larger than I expected, almost as long and fat as a pencil. Of course he had to fish them out of their biscuit tin and display their leggy crawling to Lynn, Rachel and Glynis. I didn't know girls could scream like that. Repeated throbbing blasts like an Acme thunderer whistle being given all the lung-power of a sergeant PT instructor.

After a few seconds Mr Curle's secretary came in with a note. 'Mr Otty, I am trying to interview a parent in my study. I wonder if you could keep your form a little quieter?' Reading the note to the class had much more effect than my puny efforts ever have.

But later on, there I am, trying to persuade a boy to stop squirting water with a plastic lemon. He is sitting just below the corridor window, and I am squatting down at his level, invisible to outsiders. When I suddenly stand up I must appear like a jack-in-the-box, to Mr Curle who is peering, open-mouthed through the window. When our eyes meet all I can think of doing is to give that wink, accompanied by a sideways nod of the head, and an 'ey-up?', which is a working-class street greeting. The gesture is so compelling, that Mr Curle echoes it before he is aware, and after that, all he can do is to walk away grinning.

There has been a flood disaster in the next county, and therefore we must have a rather special assembly. The deaths of several strangers rate entrance music and exit music and a long and moving address by Curle. Not wholly inappropriately we must sing 'For those in peril on the sea', and in order to ensure audibility (and because it is one of the head's favourite toys) we must have the entire ceremony amplified by a new and complicated loudspeaker system.

Everything went quite well to begin with. The pupil who was to read the lessons had a microphone round her neck, and there was another superb chrome one on a stand for the head's sermon. We all arrived safely to a musical accompaniment and we all heard every word of the lesson. But when the head tapped his mike to see if it was working before he imparted his message, the loudspeaker gave a warning crackle. Just as he is getting warmed up and is raising his voice emotionally about 'our brethren over the water', (I thought they were *under* the water) a sudden 'moo' of feedback drowns his words. He is silenced. The 'mooing' continues until he glares with such ferocity at the loudspeaker that it too shuts up. He starts again, and 'baa baa!' goes the loudspeaker. His hand shoots out and grabs the mike as though it were a reared snake in front of him. The feedback ceases, but those white knuckles, clenched round the microphone strangle his voice too and his brain also. Words shower out in choked and disconnected profusion for a minute or two, and then in desperate and tiny tones he announces the hymn.

While the school clatters to its feet and scuffles its hymn books the head scurries about on the stage fiddling with the electronics. He cures the feedback, but when we start to sing we find that he has enormously amplified his own voice. Where I am standing the volume of his voice is about equal with that of the whole of the rest of the school. He is droning an improvised bass which consists of one note repeated indefinitely with only accidental variations of pitch. The second formers who surround me will rupture something if they don't laugh aloud soon.

After the hymn he grips the mike again and confers a rather uncertain and disconnected blessing. He releases the mike, with a suspicious stare and then with pious face and tread he leaves us to contemplate his message. The piano starts up to grace his exit and stirs the mike into a final mocking bleat at his departure.

I insist that I am not being cynical either about religion or about caring for the misfortunes of others. But if values are represented by such farcical, insensitive, stupid occasions as this they fall into disrepute.

There is this feeling of apprehension attached to all the work I do at Grove End. And the physical symptoms can occur at a wide remove from the cause. Sometimes in bed on a Saturday night my stomach will come adrift from its moorings, and revolve coldly and slimily in my abdomen. Without becoming damp my hands and feet tingle with cold quicksilver sweat. And only then do I connect it with walking down the densely crowded corridor.

'Hallo sir.'

'Hallo.'

'Hallo, sir.'

'Hi, Mr Otty!'

With my heart in my Hush Puppies (because they are never so familiar with my colleagues), I reply, 'Hallo.'

So I presume all is not well. I know it. The rawest student can walk into one of these classrooms, can get the class to hear the passage they wish to read. They can give complex instructions and the children will have a go at following them. And then they get some written work which is recognizably connected with the instructions. But I, more often, get a rejection of interest.

'I'm not interested in that.' (She's more interested in a teasing and giggling game with her next-door neighbour.)

'Well, give it a try. . . . Look at this photo . . . where are they?

... what are they doing? ... why are they looking like that? ... what are they looking at, do you think?'

I slap the picture down on her desk and depart to separate the opponents in a nearby fist fight. The pupil I have just left leans over and whispers ... '?' ... what? I wonder what. Peals of laughter follow me.

There is also this very defensive feeling (have I said this before?) that if those in authority knew even as much as I do about my English lessons, they would be profoundly displeased.

And on Friday, the sort of silly incident that brings gall and heartburn. A foul taste in the mouth. 3A greeted me with a pre-arranged volley of bits of chalk. I had brought something to read to them which I am sure they would have enjoyed, but how, oh how, do you minimize such an event? Play it down and get on with the lesson, but how? And how do you reply to Peter Langland's 'How can we be good when you're so soft, sir?' I managed an unconvincing laugh, and suggested *he* tried to work out an answer. Or how do you deal with Nigel Moore's two dreary sides of writing about boomerangs? It was his first offering this term. He said: 'The old woman went on about doing some homework and I didn't want to do any of the real homework, so I wrote this.' Competent, boring, safe, dead it was too.

One small ray of hope. Hugh Evans, who looks after half of my second-form group, saw two of them playing 'hangman' at the end of registration period.

'Come along now,' says he. 'Off to your lessons.'

'Oh we're staying here for English with Mr Otty.'

'Well get out your textbooks. Put all this away.'

'But,' they said, 'we never do any work in Mr Otty's lesson.'

He asked them to show him their English books, so they proudly displayed the plays they had written for the recording sessions. Page followed page after page of play, all neatly written out.

'And you don't call this work, I suppose,' said Mr Evans. 'I think Mr Otty must be a very clever teacher!'

That was nice of him, but rather suspect. He told me himself, perhaps to cheer me up, which was kind of him. But how would Curle or Prynne react?

I don't know, but the constant dread is paralysing.

Since I seem to be keeping a fairly complete dossier on Peter Langland, I suppose I must put this sick horror in as well.

Girls

Some girls are virgins, therefore they never want to be broke in and don't go round with boys. Most of the girls I know aren't virgins, most are scrubbers. My friend amuses himself by taking his girl friend round the back of our club. All he gets from that experience is smelly fingers.

I HATE GIRLS as they can run so can't smash no windows wiv 'em about.

'Hate' is the central word. He is so eaten with hatred. How does one change that?

Growing up amongst that hatred, with her mouth shut and her eyes open, is third-form Jenny, who wrote this:

Bouquet for a Fool

This is the story of a poor girl called Sharon. She was a plain girl with no hope of a boy friend. She attended a mental check every day, because of a birth deficiency. But like most of us she dreamed a lot.

She was dreaming about a wedding, her wedding, and unknown to her she was acting the part. As it happened the local street gang was in the vicinity. When they saw her they realized that here was a source of amusement. So they listened in and they heard her say:

'Oh! What a smashing bouquet!'

Then they picked some dandelions and nettles, and they hid the nettles in the dandelions and gave them to her. Poor Sharon. She screamed, but she held onto it. She had a bouquet and she'd keep it. For the first time she held onto what little she had.

When the ambulance came the gang was still taunting her

'A bouquet, Sharon, a bouquet. Just what you wanted. A bouquet for a fool!'

I E. I found these two pieces one after the other in Alice's book.

An Old Lady

The little old lady hobbled down the street with a happy smile on her face. Her big blue eyes twinkle like stars in the sky. The little lady is getting old, her skin is wrinkled with age, her bones and veins showing, but she still hobbles down the street cheerfully. Her hair is going grey and getting finer and thinner. The little lady is only five feet in height, her legs are getting shaky and unsafe. When she sits down people come and talk to the little well-known lady. Her skin is not like the skin of a young woman, and it is dry and very soft.

Then:

Worms

Long thin slimy ones
Big fat juicy ones
Ones that squat and squirm.
We will bite their heads off
Slurp their middles out
And throw their skins away.
Nobody knows how much we thrive
On worms three times a day.

When I read the second one to the class there was quite a lot of angry talk. I eventually gathered that it is a sort of 'folk' poem, part of the oral tradition of the kids, they all knew it. And in fact Alice had got it wrong. The true version, which I didn't get hold of, had regular metre and shape.

Do I face real failure with 2B? After two days of sickness last week, when I had almost convinced myself that things were really all right, I came back to it. And the drama lesson was sheer hell. Misconceived and misbegotten with Lynn rude and sulky, getting under my skin and knowing it. Now *no* work is coming from them. Only Andrew and Mike continue to fill up exercise books with rather rubbishy James Bond-type spy fiction, working through some fantasy I can't reach. Up till now there had always been a steady trickle of writing. 3A have also given up writing. I think they are better in the classroom; at any rate as soon as I start to write about 3A a weight moves off my chest – it comes back again with a thud as soon as I realize that it only moved because I had stopped thinking about 2B! But they won't do any writing at the moment. There have been one or two occasions when it looked as though they might one day talk to each other reasonably, but write? – never.

I am not used to failure. Not since my first year at University anyway. The sick feeling in the stomach is even more intense now than it was then, and it is certainly more continuous. What is it exactly? A failed lesson breeds more failure. Failure breeds loss of confidence in me and in them and that breeds more failure. There is a language and a behaviour, and a value barrier between me and the children. The ones who cause my troubles, Lynn, Angela, Peter, Nigel, Tim, Phil, expect authority to be tough. 'Siddown and belt up', at least, if not a clip over the ear'ole.

But what they can be learning I do not know. In the meantime I dare not look beyond Grove End to imagine what failure here implies. A new job, a new career, retraining, all starting from the trough and suffering the undertow of having failed?

I am going to try a magazine with 2B. When I bravely suggest the idea to myself, it sounds as futile as launching a paper aeroplane in a hurricane . . .

But now all this discipline business is out in the open. A staff meeting at which Richard Davies (a great bearded Welsh sheep, one of the God-forsaken gwgs who have infiltrated our education) talks too loudly and too long about the state of his form-room at the end of the day.

'Chalk all over the place,' he says, 'bits of paper on the floor, paper darts, it's dreadful.'

Others join in about broken desks and writing on the walls. Jones-the-discipline declares there is no need for new rules on these points. The children must stand in the corridor until the teacher arrives.

'It's on the notice board up there.' He points. 'Obviously, if we can keep the children out of the classrooms the problem will be solved.' Grunts and bleats of agreement emerge from those broken armchairs.

Hugh Evans, loquaciously Welsh, but no gwg thank God,

pipes up. Although he is new like me, he audaciously declares that he could not disagree more. There are hisses of indrawn breath.

'If the kids were allowed to use their rooms at break and at lunchtime you'd have no problem. If they regarded the rooms as their own places where they did things and kept things they'd be more likely to respect them. I always let my classes go into the room before I get there.'

There are gasps and several knees are slapped and several jaws click open. And Jones-the-discipline feels triumphant. Pointing again at the notice board he says with the childish rhythmic emphasis with which he first drummed his two-times table into his numb skull, 'Then you are *break*ing the *rule* laid *down* on that *noticeboard* for *all* to *see*.' He adds, more quietly, and with a pitying smile 'I hope you'll forgive me for being rather blunt on this matter.' There are more cosy noises of agreement. Autonomous moral mutterings of irrefutable good sense.

'If there's a rule, it's got to be obeyed.'

'It must be the same for everyone.'

'We've got to back each other up.' And the like.

Because I feel that all this is more directed at me than at Mr Evans, I speak with my heart knocking against my ribs.

'But why must it always be the same answer? Stricter discipline. Surely the problem here is not one of vicious children and slack teachers, so why must we straightaway think in terms of punishment? I'm sure Mr Evans lets them into the rooms not because he is slack or idle, but because he thinks it is in the interests of the children and the school to do so.

'It seems to me that the real basis of the problem is an appalling building, crowded corridors, and everyone, both staff and pupils, changing rooms between classes.'

Why don't I keep my big mouth shut? I can feel the swing of people moving in support behind the opposing gwggery of Jones and Davies. Several people say there is no point in continuing the discussion. In the context they are really asserting that they are right and we are wrong. People get up muttering crossly, and the meeting is abandoned.

Evans thanked me for supporting him, another new teacher admitted agreement, but Sarah Coleman launched a vigorous attack. The substance of her argument was that free-activity methods were all right in schools in certain areas, but the Grove End children simply could not respond. They had no respect for property; they lived like that in their own homes; they would always do so; nothing could be done about it. It seems to me that if that is the case teaching becomes a kind of police action, a matter of containment. We suppress most of the kids, spout at them continuously and hope something will adhere to a minority who can go to the university and then return to suppress and spout at another generation. And if that is the case, then it is a profession for mugs (and gwgs).

Then I become aware that Richard Davies is approaching, thrusting his pubic beard at me, and winding up his clockwork eloquence.

'Now look, Mr Otty, your teaching methods are no concern of mine. What you do in the classroom is of no interest to me.' (How true! I think.) Then he starts to gesture, counting off point by point on fingers held under my nose.

'If you want to have (one) free-expression lessons which involve moving all the desks, it's quite all right by me (arms spread wide, shoulders shrugged).

If you want to have (two) free-expression lessons in which all the kids throw chalk at one another, it's (arms spread wide) all right by me.

If you want to have (the third counting gesture is so close that I flinch back a nervous pace) free-expression lessons which involve making paper darts, it's (shoulders shrugged) all right by me.

Only (he wags a choppy chalky forefinger), *please* (intoned with an ironic whine of appeal) *please* see that they clean up afterwards.'

So I am sick in the guts tonight and can't see my way to any work or thought beyond my disgrace. Commenting on the meeting, a red-faced geography master, who was nervously hitting the back of his head with a squash-racquet, declared that his fifth form had told him that the only teacher they liked and respected was the one who never let them say a word or do anything at all.

'They do, you know, they respect you for it, they gain a sense of security from a rigid form of discipline.' Etcetera, etcetera, etcetera in circles.

Big pause ... deep breath ... I have been to see Michael Cohen, and I have talked with him and his wife about Grove End. I told them about the staff meeting and they were sympathetic. I told them about the hairy gwg's attack, and they were appalled. They neatly framed their understanding of Grove End in words which assured me that they had taken my meaning, and at the same time they somehow made me reassess that meaning myself.

Over the staff's determination to keep the kids out of the classrooms, Michael said – 'That's it. It's the oldest repressive argument of them all. The slippery slope! "Give them an inch", they say, "and they'll take an ell." The feeling is that if you let the kids do *anything* which was formerly prohibited then the next thing will be that they're taking over the west wing, and there are barricades and barbed wire in the playground.'

Rather to my surprise, they both said with a kind of abrupt certainty, that if it was really that kind of a school, I should get out of it as soon as possible. This set me to wondering if it was really *that* kind of a school. Am I exaggerating?

However, an advertisement has appeared, opportunely, for a post at the local public school, and I am going to apply. I have already met the head of English and looked over the school. The differences between it and Grove End are dramatic. The buildings are nineteenth-century Gothic. They are ill-suited to teaching (or indeed to human habitation), but they transmit certain values without a word being said. They declare with their massive expensiveness that the institution they house is important, is cherished and admired. They are uncomfortable and ugly and draughty, and in some ways ill equipped when compared to a state school, but the greensward, the Doric portico of the cricket pavilion, the chapel and the hall and the cloisters make the passer-by stop and wonder what that building is, wonder what goes on there, and who is allowed past the war memorial gate.

It is imaginative to spend your financial resources on an environment which expresses the notion that it cares about what goes on there. I don't mean that what public schools do is necessarily good. It's just that when you enter the grounds all the buildings whisper that they mean business. Public schools are effective. The output at the end of the process is different from the input – and in ways which can be readily attributed to the school. Grove End, on the other hand, expresses our society's attitude to state education. It is still a charity. There, the buildings mutter: 'You are being done on the cheap and are lucky to be done at all.'

Now, although I went to a public school myself, I feel deeply divided at the idea of applying for a job in one. On the one hand it would be a relief. It would be returning to my world, where, when people ask what I do and I say I teach, they politely assume that it must be at a university or at a public school. They find it a socially uncomfortable fact that I teach in a school they have never even heard of. But now I am becoming grimly convinced that there is something wrong with educating the inhabitants of that world in a separate exclusive enclave. It seems to me that the people who quietly run this country, not necessarily those who govern, but those who are in a position to shape the priorities of government, tend to be the ones who use the public schools. While that is so, they can afford to regard Grove End as a marginal kind of establishment. There is no conscious suppression of the masses, or anything like that, it is just that state education need not be taken very seriously by the people with money and power, because their children will not have to share it.

Anyway, I am going to apply. They probably won't want me, which will save my little conscience

I mentioned hate in connection with Peter Langland's last piece. Look at this one:

People Who I Hate in this Class

I hate Gordon small because he's a little punk. He wears gert boots 'cause he had an accident when he was a little baby. I wish the bloody lorry killed him. He's a little baby, I bunged his PT kit down the loo and he opened his gert mouth to head-slapper Jones (the teacher with the gert big nose).

I also hate Moloney. He got a gert fat gut on him, and in rugby he's scared of the ball let alone the bloody players.

I also hate Farmyard (Farmer) he's a dirty fink and you could grow cabbages behind his ears and go coal mining down his neck.

Jenny is a fat flat-chested turd, and Anne (the cow) is a swine. She split on Philip when Ethel asked the class who had been chucking stuff about.

I do like Mr Otty sometimes.

The ending almost makes me weep! What can it mean after all that boiling hatred? And after all that seething chaos caused by Peter in the classroom?

2B's newspaper is something of a success. It has taken two weeks to produce two sides of printed foolscap, which is pretty inefficient use of thirty-seven potential journalists, but it did actually happen. Dick and Robert, who have been engaged in spy stories up till now, were touchingly industrious. After school they worked away counting every letter and space and punctuation mark in every article so that we could plan the layout accurately. A splinter group of five formed, who insisted that they would make their own magazine, but apart from these five, the entire class felt involved in the publication. They read it through from cover to cover (that is, both sides) and they now want to do one with six sides, and sell it for the next charity collection. Dick and Robert interviewed Mr Peters, the new senior master, which I thought was rather courageous of them. No one on the staff has proved brave enough to talk to him yet. They just complain about him in the common room, so when some nosey old bag found a copy of the 2B Times in my pigeonhole, word got around and the whole staff were to be seen furtively reading it and passing it on. This was really good for me: I could smile knowingly on the sidelines, and then acknowledge that what they had been so avidly consuming had been produced in one of my disciplineless English lessons.

Conversation with Miss Prynne
The topic is Nigel Moore of 3A.

'Oh, Mr Otty, there is something I've been meaning to mention to you about homework. Now some of our naughty boys are put on homework report, and their parents do their weak best to see that these ones do get something done. But apparently they say to Moore, "What is your English homework, it's down on the timetable for tonight", and he can say "Oh, there's none set."

'Well of course this looks bad, doesn't it? If they are, as I say, doing their weak best and it turns out that there is no homework set, it looks as though it's the school that is being slack.

'Now Moore has always been a bit of a problem. Right from the word go he had to be chased up for homework. And apparently, as his parents tell me, he was the only boy in the street who was going to the grammar school, and as none of the others had homework, he said he wasn't going to do homework. So you see what it amounts to is that the parents have been slack for three years.'

– But Nigel is leaving school at the earliest possible moment. He is doing the third-year course for the second time. At present he seems to be incapable of doing valuable work under the most favourable conditions. He pays Biggs sixpence a week to do his music homework (old Hopkins is very strict), and he runs a general advice service on his best subject, which is French. He wants to join the Army Catering Corps. But, nevertheless, in this situation he must now as a first step towards redeeming the total failure of his grammar-school education, be coerced into doing his homework. And therefore he must have homework set in case the school appears to be slack. It's not just slack, it is flaccid.

I wriggled out of it somehow. I used words like socialization, and the internalization of the achievement ethic, and exploring the environment into which he is so soon to move, and I left Miss P. puffing through her pout.

a picturepoem.

```
superterrificsmashingqwertyuiopasdfghjkl;zxcvbnm,.123456789-qwerty.
uiopasdfghjkl;,zxcvbnm,.qwertyuioplkjhgfdsasdertfvbnhyutgfredswasd
yujkilhtrewqasedfvg  fghjuytrewsedfghjuikloiuyhnm,kjhgfcvbnvcssdavd
uytcgfdssaghhjjkn    aiuytrfghjjbvdsadfghjkllknbfddertfcc  tyuioplk
hellohowareyouhy     yuiopiuytredfghhytrewdfcghvbnm  iukzxcvxzoxds
jujuyuikloikiuy      7yte48iuyhl-klku jxyuhjgtdfresdrghjko,mrs
ochdontdothatyc      naughtyboyghjkliutcewsdfahhjuytfgredsdf
bewarethe ja         berwockmysonthejawsthatbitetheclaw
sthatsnat            chbewarethe jubjubbirdandshunthef
rumiousb             andersnatchooooooooohjohnpeel,
yousetus             llonfireyouaresoevocativesoredicu
louslytoom           chinfactyouareratherniceghjkliuytrew
itsnottruei          snottrueitsnottrueitsnottrueitsnottrue
aftertheli           ghtsgooutasmallmachinehascomecreeping
intomylife           pleasegivemeonemorechanceorhaveiasked
tnistoooft           entorealisethatireallyreallyreally e
allyreally           eallymeanitquestionmarkprettyboygir
eusakissth           enwhosaprettyprettyboynotyouwhatthe
ieildoyouthi         nkiam,sexstarvedorsomethingquestion
mark"somecunt        hasknockedmyfuckingbike"writtenon
awallinashel         terinthepark(whichirefusedtosay)it
mskesyousow          eraboutthereprodutivehabitsofbi
cycleSalsoc          aboutthephysicalimpossibilitiesof
thewholef            ckingphrasewhatlynne,swearingatyo
urage...             youweredrunklastsaturday,werentyo
uquestionh           arktinytimohtinytimyouhavecaptured
dmyhea               howiloveyourlonghairandyourukel
eleoh      inyt      imhowiloveyouandilltiptoethrough
hetu       lipswi    thyouanydayandillkiss(ooooooooh)
you        inthega   rdenifyoullpardonmeooohinspirat
io         nforapoe  m,thoughtstosendhomeonapicture
p  p       ostcard,w onderingwhetherornottosayilove
y  b       oubutineve rdsoidontknowwhyiworryaboutit
ou         utido,ju  stincaseonedayitshouldjustslip
ou         tandiwi   llbelostlostlostbecausesometh
ct         ghttha    snotoccuredtoyouhowcouldiexpe
.ill       it,e      eciallyfromaboylikeyouwelli
foodm      fo        rgetyouandlovetinytimxxxxxxx
'Carry               rninggoodmorninggoodmorning!
andispl              onapussycathascomeintomyroom
ngthekey             ayingwiththetypewriterpatti
rmedhowwonc          andattackingthewordsbeingfo
xtweekimgot          erfullymagic!!!!sometimene
autifhlsuit          gintobristoltobuythemostbe
roundthewa           withvneck,crossovertop,belt
ithadarkred          stinsilkynavybluematerialw
fantastican          distripeandanavyblueskirtitis
ohifeelverylo        itonlycosts£3:19:11d!!!!!!!
mustntfeeldow   n    elybecausel,ehasnotphonedbuti
ethat(ordoit}        nbecauseidontlovehimoranythinglik
stolove,which        imustwatchoutincaseloneliness lea
thesorttofall        wouldbeabigmistakebecauseheisnot
careenoughto         inlovewithme...atthemomentidont
meoneelse-u          besupset,butimustlookaround orso
chishighly           nlesshedoeseventuallyphone,whi
                     Punlikelyoh,ifeelsosad ometimes."
```

But then fourth form Fiona gave me this. It is so beautiful, and the words are not just background; they really are worth decyphering. Unfortunately I feel I cannot rush off and show it to Miss Prynne as a piece of unsolicited homework, because there are two 'rude' words in the middle. I'm afraid she would not appreciate it.

The headmaster of our local public school has thanked me for my application, and was sorry to have to inform me that the post has now been filled.

I later heard on the grape-vine, that the successful application was an Oxbridge first, and a half-blue in squash. As the head of department said, the school was looking for someone rather special, and frankly he thought it deserved someone rather special.

2B Lynn is a most extraordinary person. Ignoring the magazine, today, first of all she pleads with me for an idea for some writing. I am too busy with the arguing, scrambling and complaining of the rest of the form to offer any suggestions. So she grabs a piece of paper, and with a fierce concentration which excludes everyone else in the room she writes this:

Industry

Tapp!tapp! machines faster!
Gloved hands busy working!
Mechanical means worked
By its master
Tapp! tapp! machines faster!

Nuts – bolts – machines faster
Unknown to the Dumb
Outcaster
Iron teeth, jaws
Rhythm,
Tapp! tapp! machines faster!

Tapp! tapp! machines faster!
Unseen by the dumb outcaster
Automatic clock-work rhythm.
Tapp! tapp! machines faster!

What on earth can she mean by 'the dumb outcaster'? It sounds like some device at the very end of the assembly line – it also sounds like a kind of 'immanent will'!

3A. Simon Farmer (the 'Farmyard' on whose neck Peter Langland thinks we could grow cabbages) is really only interested in football. Up until now he has written nothing but football commentaries. This is called:

The Dark Night

As night sets in on the industrial town of Sheffield, nearly all is quiet. The only thing that stirs in the night is the whistle of the trains as they go by.

The river is peaceful, and I listened to the ripples of the river, although it was filthy and there was still dead fish on the surface.

The first factory I came to was a steel plant with soot over its huge walls. I heard clip clop, clip clop, as the night watchman did his rounds. At this time of night Sheffield is at its best with no smoke to fill the air. The side streets were filthy and full of rubbish.

The moon shone down on the inadequately lighted streets. I walked on, listening for any sound, when I heard a person singing round the corner.

I walked round to see a man with a shabby coat swaying with a bottle of gin. He had a round face and a scar on his cheek. I walked past in amazement at the state of the poor devil. I looked up and saw the moon.

I then thought of London with its slums, but the buildings could not be as black as these. I decided to take a shorter route to the bus station.

It is not a remarkably good piece of writing. What is extraordinary about it is the difference in tone between it and its author's standard approach to life. He is a rough. He hates poetry, he reads nothing, he is always fighting, and when he talks to you he is always pushing his dialect further and further from 'education English'.

4E. How about this splendid evocation of the brown world of the grammar school? Our Friday morning assemblies of eight-hundred pupils are referred to, by Mr Curle, as the

Family Gathering

... Bunching down the dark low muttering corridor, past the row of hawk-eyed reprimanding staff. Stepping into the light, wide, chaired hall, shrinking with arrivers. Squiggling into close rows of black, tinny railed chairs, whispering or untalking, they're all scrunching in, sitting on chairs, floors, everywhere.

Now we wait with eyes and rustling. Everyone stares round, around, stopping, looking, staring, up and down.

Then the Figure sweeps into our midst – a wave of rustling standing-up sweeps throughout. Voice tells you 'Hymn 258 . . .' Some black piano tune rings out and teachers tune up. Brave staff stole away while pupils mumble a colourless backing, if they can see a book. Boys from the third form upwards can't.

The reader blushes, speaks, is interrupted, starts again. No pupil listens; all stare, eye, gawp at haircuts, shoes, skirts, new boy, new girl. Bored routine. Prayers to give thanks for a lovely morning – The Figure thinks we ought to. Small poisonous voice from behind, 'He thinks. He thinks. Nothing happens here but *he* thinks.' Old-worded flowery prayers pour haughtily forth, once beautiful. Every pupil titter-giggle is rustling out all the long weird words and the little first-form boy in the middle actually *closes his eyes*!

End of assembly. Staff rise hesitantly and follow The Figure out – the only coloured people amongst our brown mass. Many, many we pour out into a sunlight mottled corridor and talk our way back up . . .

I have been digging out tree-stumps this weekend. It ought to be boring work but in my present state of mind I love it. For one thing it confers a guaranteed honourable exhaustion which I can assume to be virtuous. Very different from my guilty twitching after a school day! And then, where the problems of teaching are so complex and intractable, the objects of manual labour can usually be obtained with perseverance and hard work – those educational panaceas so beloved of report writers.

When digging out a stump, I can plan ahead. If I dig a deep hole here I can rake the earth from the roots into it. If I start this side rather than that it will offer certain advantages. No matter how complicated the roots, I can win in the end.

But with teaching, the aims and the methods are impossibly complex and interwoven, because teaching is the whole business of communication, and because that is so complex and frustrating. There is so much more than the words one speaks or writes. Particularly in a school, I think, there are one's allegiances. We communicate by what we are, by what we really feel. You can say, 'shut up', and convey in one context a desire to close off all channels of thought, and in another, the same words carry a confidence in a relationship which leads out to new things, as one might say it to a valued friend. All those mysterious human connections are there, the twists of meaning and logic, and the ambivalence of relationships, and one stumbles over the paradoxical moments when something is learned, days, months, years after they occurred unnoticed. One snaps any tender growing fibre at one's peril.

The day after a discussion with 3A about punishment and discipline, Peter Langland handed in this:

How I Think the School Should be Run

My views about how this school as it is now is that I shall be glad when I leave. Before, when Mr Daniels was here, I enjoyed the school. I didn't mind when there were detentions after school but now with black marks it's terrible. How I think this school should be run.

1. Abolish black marks, instead have nightly detentions.
2. If one gets a Saturday morning detention he or she should have the choice of either three nightly detentions or six whacks.
3. There should be more representatives at the school council and these should not be afraid to speak up for themselves.
4. There should also be a suggestion box for pupils.

5. One could drop these lessons if one wants to: 1) Latin
2) Music 3) Art and as substitute do more French, Maths
or English.
6. Mr Jones should either be more fair or be put as an
ordinary teacher and someone else take his place (I state
this as Mr Jones never believes your side of the story,
always believes the prefects or the staffs.)
7. There should be less homework.
8. Instead of having games, P.T. Art and Metalwork on
different days of the week we should have: first double Art,
then double metalwork and then all afternoon games.

Well, he has made a terrific effort to be fair: not an obscenity,
not even a 'bloody gert', not a single 'ponce' or 'scrubber', not
even a staff nickname. Some points which have a lot in them, 3,
4, 5, 6, 7. I don't understand No. 8 at all, unless he is trying to
establish one day in the week which he is bound to enjoy. I think
it is a real achievement, but it is difficult to give it the recognition
which I think it deserves because of the just, but directly personal
attack on Jones.

Anyway, what about the second-form magazine? In the end we
got three editions out – the first had two sides, the others six. The
content of the first two was a curious mixture of news copied out.
e.g.

'Every year no less than 2000 walrus spend their holiday
on one small beach all crowded together. Because they
spend so much of their time on land it causes their
temperature to rise and makes their bodies go bright
pink.'

Articles roughly transcribed from various sources, 'Your
Stars', a pop column called 'Charlie's Chat', and so on. With the
third we got some good stories and an excellent article by Jonathan on unusual pets, all about a racket he used to organize
selling toads and frogs to gullible acquaintances. At the suggestion of Lynn, we sold editions two and three, and raised nearly
three pounds for the Lent charity.

The best moments were the Friday morning lessons when I
arrived after a fortnight of mixed murder with the printed copies
of the completed magazine.

Perhaps the most impressive thing of all was the series of front-page interviews with members of staff. These were always read with great delight by the teachers.

But ... over the six weeks which these three editions took to make, far too few of the class were actively involved and far too much time was wasted. I was so busy I could not speak to anyone who was not interested in the project. Harris took a liking to the idea, but he took an aversion to the people who were doing it. He said he was going to run his own paper, and I, seeing visions of my own work doubling overnight, made vaguely discouraging noises. I didn't see him for a fortnight or so, and then he appeared one day with two typed skins ready for duplicating, the Grove End Gazette, Editor J. Harris.

He had written and typed almost the entire edition himself. The others were very critical of his efforts, but they became more reconciled when he offered to do some typing for the final edition of the official form magazine.

With work like this, it would be an enormous help if there were an English room – like the Art room – in which to work. Then there could be a table, or a corner, or a wall where the newspaper people could get together and work, and one would have a better chance of dealing with the rest of the group. Since I teach 2B in five different rooms during the week, and since there is no equipment or space in any of these rooms, it is not surprising that not all that happens can be dragged under the English umbrella.

There is, for example a curious version of football which they play with three coins and a ruler on a desk-top. It's rather like billiards. The trouble is that it keeps second formers quietly occupied for quite long stretches of time, and if any of my second form are quiet and orderly I'm likely to leave them to it! There is no effective way of stopping it except, I suppose, by punishing its every appearance. But in that case what was I to do with Dick and Robert? They have worked with me after school every night this week, for forty minutes or an hour, counting letters and spaces and planning the layout. Then, on Friday while the paper was being enthusiastically stapled together and read by the class, they, who know its contents, backwards, decide to refresh themselves with a game of desk-top football.

It seems so just and so natural.

Summer term

I had ended last term with some feelings of triumph. If the behaviour of 2B was still pretty poor, they had at least produced the newspaper. In the school concert I had played a bit of a string quartet with three sixth formers, and that gained me a certain prestige in some very unlikely quarters. But the very first lesson with 3B this term was an appalling failure to communicate and following up some vague and edgy threats I at last gave out a bunch of black marks that would have delighted the gwggery. Anne Dixon suggested that I should keep them in the corridor until I was ready for them, and let them into the classroom one by one separating out the troublesome group. The result was a spectacular reduction of noise. Only Lynn and Angela really resisted the new atmosphere. But I don't like the new feel of the lessons. I have transferred some of the tension from me to them. They are wary like they were at the very beginning of the year.

My new disciplinarian pose with 2B is already on the crumble. It is such an unconvinced pose I cannot maintain it. I tried to shore it up with exam blackmail:

'We have exams soon after half term, and I think we ought to have a look at the kinds of thing you will be asked to do.'

Of course they are just as good at the blackmail as I am!

'If I fail my exams, sir, it will be your fault for not keeping us under control.'

Rita wrote the following for her practice:

Q.1 *View from a Cliff*

Below me lay the rolling pitching sea. The rocks were one mass of foaming, frothing white. It bubbled and boiled like a witches cauldron. Above me was a peaceful blue sky dotted here and there with a few clouds. The grass below

my feet was soft and cool. Around me was wind, pretty
rough wind.

Gulls were wheeling and crying around me. I was alone.
The wind was making the sea rough. As you looked down
there was nothing but turmoil below. As you fell down
there was nothing but blackness.

Q.2 *Before a Storm*
The sky was black and threatening,
The air was calm and still,
The sky was split with lightning.
Then the thunder came
Again and again and again.
The lightning flashed,
The thunder roared,
The wind sprung up in anger.
Then the calm came again,
The storm was over.
No more lightning flashed
No more thunder roared,
The wind was calm, not anger.

I have written a compo and a poem

Rita.

While Rita was writing this, Fiona and Angela came to violent
blows a few feet away. Angela rushed from the room and spent
the rest of the morning weeping. Fiona was unrepentant until the
house staff 'talked it over with her'. After that she spent most of
the afternoon in tears.

Peter Langland in more characteristic vein has produced this:

My Ambition
I would like to be a multi-millionaire, and have a road-
racing course, and a scramble course, and a Greeves 650
c.c. for tracking, and a Triumph Bonsville for road racing
and a vintage car for driving about. I would also like a
stock-car track, and be able to have an E type Jag, for that
sport.

I would buy a speed boat and a luxury cruiser and be able to run twenty casinos and anyone who owed me money would get shot. I would like to be WORLD'S PUBLIC ENEMY–NO. 1.

I would be a thousand times worse than Al Capone.

I would get married and have my fun then kill her and then buy a hundred brothels. And I'd buy thirty strip clubs.

Horrifying, and rather fascinating, to see this mad progression in his mind set out on paper. Motor-bikes, cars, speedboat, cruiser, money, gambling, violence, sex and the desire to shock and to repel. Why? I have seen him doing it among his peers too. Telling some story that goes beyond their stomachs leaving them deeply disgusted and rather admiring.

I'm sure it is an unconscious reaction to Peter's determined efforts to be horrible, that causes half his trouble with the staff. They even say things like,

'I can put up with naughty boys, but Langland is somehow different. He's disgusting.'

Well, he is disgusting. Most of what he has written for me has had an underlying determination to disgust and repel. He uses all his experience of school life to produce tones of voice, expressions of the face, gestures, which get right under the schoolmasterly skin. It is this disgust and revulsion that gives the real emotional force to the staff's moral condemnation of Peter.

There is another boy in the third year, who gets just as many black marks as Peter or Nigel, but his role in relation to the staff is that of an attractive clown. Everybody likes him, and as was said at a recent staff meeting, they make a special case of him because they are sure that he will one day be a valuable member of the school. I don't mind that. The more special treatment the better. But the kids who make themselves difficult to like, and who need liking, and whose future contribution to the school we are not at all sure about, really need the positive and affectionate special treatment. Surely that must be so. Otherwise we are simply using our disgust as a justification for washing our hands of them. One would not do that with a cancer patient.

What about this for an English homework from fourth form Fiona!

Le temps est gris,
C'est froid ici
Les oiseaux ne chantent pas souvent.
Il n'y a pas de rossignol:
Je ne vois qu'un corbeau sur une branche noire,
Contre le ciel gris.
C'est froid ici,
Ou je t'attends.

Why is it so difficult to talk about Grove End outside school? Who wants to admit that they might be failing? You can see people turning away emotionally as they do from disabled people! It is easiest, I find, to stick to the idiocies of 'the system'. It is not hard to talk disparagingly about the different stupidities I have encountered. But I even shy away from talking to Sue about some of my thoughts about school. I don't want her to know just how panicky I am. She does know, of course, and when we do talk she brings a splendid fiery kind of reassurance to me. She makes all kinds of imaginative threats about what she'd do to the poor fools who don't appreciate me. And that's a great help, though the vividness of the threats makes me feel I must have been unfair about my colleagues.

It is also good swapping stories with Tom and Michael Cohen. They both give the impression of having been honourably scarred in the profession, of having fought genuinely similar battles, and of having come through them. And then the stories themselves build up a kind of living composite map of the battlefield. One can take a story and chew over its implications, its resonances, its parallels with other incidents. The stories give form and body to my more general notions of how I can and should carry on.

The worst moments are when people offer sympathetic advice about what to do, when they don't and can't know what situation they are speaking into. There is a belief among teachers that if you start to talk about discipline it must be because you want to *get* discipline – discipline conceived of as a set of relatively simple skills. And then they are not really fighting the same battle, they are not even looking in the same direction.

I suppose I feel I need a lot of simple, emotional, personal support. But I don't want to ask for it, of course.

As I mentioned earlier, our understanding of the nature of language seems to me to show quite convincingly that language is not a habit structure, but that it has a kind of creative property, and is based on abstract formal principles and operations of a complex kind. My own feeling is that from our knowledge of the organization of language and of the principles that determine language structure, one cannot immediately construct a teaching programme. All we can suggest is that a teaching programme be designed in such a way as to give free play to those creative principles that humans bring to the process of language learning, and I presume to the learning of anything else. I think we should probably try to create a rich linguistic environment for the intuitive heuristics that the normal human automatically possesses.

Noam Chomsky, talking to Stuart Hampshire.

What about 2B? There seems to be something in my chemistry which rubs them up the wrong way. When a child starts to annoy me deliberately I try to reason with him. But that's not what he wants. He wants first of all the success of the exploit he has undertaken, i.e. getting me annoyed. These days, with the creeping anxiety in my belly, I am ashamed to confess they sometimes succeed. Worse, they make me despair and give up.

After I have prepared several lessons with that group in mind, talked myself into an amiable disposition, refused to be upset by them for several days, and there is still no change, and the next time I take something to them I am greeted with moans and jeers and a refusal to listen, I find the whole day goes sour. I am counting the days, hours, lessons to half-term, to the end of term, to my release.

With 3A I find I have learned something and they have learned something, though this may just be passage of time. 2B is just a passport to a chaotic hell, however. I am only interested in what the difficult ones write, and then only because of the way it relates to how they behave. I am beginning to think I don't want to teach first and second forms. I don't want to have anything to do with these masks of role-playing which they adopt as they struggle with their inner turmoil. Certainly it seems that a school day of forty-five minute lessons in irrelevance, is an educational failure for them. And yet it is because of what happens at this stage that the sheep and the goats are separated at this school!

The worst thing is that I am led by these failures, to blow pipe-dreams about the future. I imagine a job that will give me more time to myself, leave me more energy for my spare time, and, most of all, a job which will boost rather than sap my morale, my *amour propre*. Perhaps liberal studies at a technical college would offer more direct emotional returns?

And so on. And the realization of what I am doing in my mind, and the relaxation of my nerves when I imagine myself in such a post, and the contempt I feel for my feebleness, all continue to sap and undermine that morale and *amour propre*.

Another family gathering.

'Now I have, now, you must, you must all know what I am talking about. There are some among us, and I don't, there are some, some people think it is amusing to . . .

You there.

No, you with the fair hair,

You seem to think it's funny.

STAND UP!

No. Not you, the next boy.

You can all . . . you seem to . . . there he is . . .

LOOK at him.

All right, sit down again.

I have a word or two to say about a symbol. It may not mean, to you who are so much younger, you may not realize. A symbol of evil.

You just think it might be fun to, when you have nothing better to do, and even, I think, I think these silly football games which ought to stop now the cricket season is here, even football is better.

You take some chalk, and incidentally I don't know where you think it comes from. The chalk in this school is not for your games but for ours.

But for those of you, of us who lived through the last war and saw the rise of evil. You may not realize. And all I've got to say to you is – It's got to stop.

Now will you all turn and look at the stage.
ALL RIGHT, YOU CAN BRING IT ON.'

The whole school turns towards the closed crimson curtains with the spotlit circle in the centre. Two boys emerge carrying a blackboard on which a huge swastika has been drawn. The tableau, the confrontation between crowd and symbol, has atmosphere, but of what kind?

For a moment I can almost believe that we will all shout 'Sieg Heil! Sieg Heil!'

Steve Burton, in the fourth form, hides behind aliases. All his work contains a twist of the idea, it is ironical and involved though not always successful. The cover of his exercise book is decorated in a pattern of rubber stamps BURTON, BURTON, BURTON, but superimposed in heavy ball point is 'this book belongs to Fred Blogs'. The word English is cut out in inch high letters upside down ITDNƎ on the front cover, and HS on the back. Each piece of work has a copyright sign at the end © Steven Burton 1968, or else he writes a poem and at the end puts 'by Thomas Hardy 1840–1928'.

Here he is winding up for an Eng. Lit. essay on *Great Expectations*.

Lundi dix-huite mai
Une SA
by Steven Burton
Based on an idea by Nick Otty
From the book by Charles Dickens
Great Expectations
The changes in Pip's attitude towards Joe.

Here's a piece by Paul: very evocative of the dinginess of our profession.

The teacher has gone away
The one I long for . . .
. . . to fall in a hole . . .
. . . or to be swallowed up . . .
Maybe his moolies will fall off.
Ha, ha, hee, hee.

Poor chap . . . no fun in his life . . . no regrets . . . no kids
either
Only boiled spinach and clocks
Tick tock, tick tock
Click clocks, Click clocks
On and on to eternity or . . .
. . . or until that dreaded day, that tortuous occasion, when
by some unknown hand, fate strikes and the main spring
breaks.

Down, down to retirement. No more putting on an hour
for summer time. Just rust, rust, more rust, and even more
rust.

The 2B chaos has produced *one* piece of good writing and
alarmingly shrewd observation.

The Teacher's Nightmare
Part One

The scene is set in the teachers' room. They are all taking
pills and drinking whisky to calm their nerves.

One of the teachers leaves the room and goes to the
headmaster. He knocks on the door and the HM tells him
to come in.

HM Good morning, Mr —, I hope you haven't come
about teaching 2B.

TEACHER (getting down on his knees and begging to
the HM)
Please, headmaster, please don't make me teach 2B. I'll
do anything, anything, but please, headmaster, have a
heart. I teach 2B, go home, get to sleep and start having
nightmares about them. Please, headmaster. (He breaks
under the strain and sinks to the ground sobbing.)
The headmaster starts pulling at his hair or what's left
of it and starts stamping around.

HM (in a loud voice) I've had enough. I'm resigning.
You're the fifth teacher to come to resign after teaching
2B. Please stay.

TEACHER But what about Miss—. She went to teach 2B
and look where she is now.

HM Yes, are you going to the funeral?

TEACHER No. But that poisoned dart did the trick.

HM We've got to think of something.

(Back in the teachers' room.)

MR A. Well it's been nice knowing you old boy. I hope you make it.

MR B. I'll try. Give me a glass. (He is handed a half pint mug, and he fills it with whisky. Into it he puts a dozen pills. His hand is shaking and he is going grey, though he is only twenty-five or twenty-six. He picks up the concoction and where his hand is shaking he spills it over his shirt. He drinks the rest with a gulp.) Okay, Mr A, fit me out.

MR A. Well, there's a gas gun, smoke bomb, tin helmet, gas mask, luger, machine gun and death pill.

MR B. No bullet proof vest? No riot control shield?

MR A. No, sorry chum. Well, you're on your own for the next forty minutes. Goodbye.

MR B. Goodbye (he speaks with a heavy heart). Tell my wife I want an oak coffin and a wreath of roses.

End of Part One

That's all very jolly. It is too grotesque for the reader to have to take it very seriously, though it only slightly caricatures the embattled feeling of our staff meetings, 'We must have a real all out campaign about corridor discipline, etc.'

Part two, being more realistic, was much more difficult to take!

The Teacher's Nightmare
Part Two Journey into Death

MR B. slowly trudged up the corridor to Room G. He stopped, took a deep breath, and said 'Go in 2B!'

But there was no one there, they had already gone in. He took another deep breath, entered the room and said, 'Good morning 2B.' But his voice was drowned by the boos and jeers.

'Boo, Booo. Ha ha ha.'

He tried again.

'GOOD MORNING'

BOY Good afternoon, Mr B.

MR B. I thought we might read a passage from this book.
It is called *Old Mali and the Boy*.

GIRL Oh no! Everything you read is boy's books. My
dad says that ... (she was cut off)

BOY Ah shut up. We know what your – Dad says. 'You
ought to do this. We ought to do that.'

ANOTHER BOY Why don't he take a running
jump?

ANOTHER BOY Aw, come on sir, let's get on wiv it.

MR B. Silence. Shush ... quiet, Angela.

GIRL I won't shut up and you can't make me.

MR B. Now look, Angela, show some manners.

BOY Yeah, show some manners, stupid cow. Hurry up
and start, sir.

MR B. Lynn, will you stop combing Simon's hair. This
is an English lesson. Well, it's supposed to be an English
lesson. Richard will you stop messing about with
Lynn.

BOY Yeah, Rich., stop it.

RICHARD (with mouth agape, idiot fashion) Aw, sir, I
wuz only messin about.

CLASS Oy, Oy! messing about with her were you?

RICHARD Aw shut up. Why can't you stop making
those wet jokes? You're a SPAZ.

MR B. That's enough! Now let's get on with the
reading.

A loud laugh comes from the back of the room.

MR B. Quiet! (then, to someone near him)
Why can't they do something constructive for a change?
But all you get is Lynn combing Simon's hair, and
Michael shouting, and that mob in the corner reading
Batman and Superman comics.

A paper dart whizzes past and hits the blackboard with a
thud. Pause.

MR B. WHO DID IT? Right, if I don't get silence, I'll
give you all black marks.

BOY Cum orf it, sir. You're too soft.

ANOTHER BOY It was a good try, but you're just too soft.

ANOTHER You might as well give up.

ANOTHER They know you won't give them black marks.

MR B. Well, you know, I don't really believe in punishment. RIGHT, Angela you've got a black mark!

ANGELA Well, that's not – fair! I ain't – done nothing. It's not fair. Anyway I couldn't care less. And anyway, my dad reckons he ought to give out more black marks than he does.

BOY Shut up, Angela.

ANGELA I won't shut up!

MR B. Now, Angela, please keep quiet.

ANGELA I won't shut up! You can't make me.
(The bell goes and the lesson ends.)

CLASS HURRAYYYY!!

MR B. Oh Hell! (He starts to pack away the books in his briefcase.) Stop climbing out of the windows. I give up! I don't know what to do. I honestly don't.

BOY Well, sir, (with a grin) what will we get away with next lesson?

The end

The realism contrasts strongly with the fantasy of part 1. The detached, ironical observation is disturbing in a second former. That is to say, I don't see how a teacher can adopt a role which pretends that the children can't see him and his motives as clearly as this.

The little horror! My first reaction to reading the piece was 'Can I persuade him to burn this exercise book'!

Quote from a sixth-form Chaucer essay:
The Summoner is an ugly man who indulges in sexual impropriety:
'As hoot he was and lecherous as a sparwe'.

What vigorous insight.

I have not mentioned the sixth form since I came to Grove End. I think this is because there is no survival factor about my lessons with them. I recently asked them to give an account of their experience of Shakespeare with some very interesting results. For example:

I had my first real contact with Shakespeare when I was at junior school. An over-optimistic teacher (student perhaps?) decided that we would enjoy reading *Macbeth*, and we were made to struggle through the first two or three acts. I could not understand it, and disliked it intensely except for the witches. By the age of eleven I had decided that I hated the man and everything he wrote.

The prejudice was not helped by the fact that our first year in the senior school was 1964, the 400th anniversary of Shakespeare's birth. Luckily we managed to escape reading any of his plays but we were told his life story in great detail, and the school trip that year was to the Shakespeare museum at Stratford. This did not make much impression on me. I can remember only that it was very dark, rather confusing, and full of black and white modern art. I can remember much more clearly Woolworth's soggy sandwiches and melted ice-cream.

The next attempt to make me realize that he was the greatest playwright who ever lived, was a revolting little book called *Little Plays from Shakespeare*. For this various short scenes were chosen, chopped and censored, from selected plays. It also gave a precis of the plot. His plays usually depend more on dialogue and character than on plot, and this was not very encouraging. For example:

'The king prepares poison for Hamlet which the Queen drinks by mistake, and dies, Laertes confesses and dies, and Hamlet kills the king and dies'.

That deprives the scene of any meaning or beauty it might have had.

Once I forced my father to watch the film of Romeo and Juliet on the television. He remained unconverted and still refers to that – Shakespeare who writes a load of —₂ —₂ rubbish.

Shakespeare must be a genius to survive the assaults of our education! It is a pity the kids see his survival as a successful plot organized by examiners and teachers.

Peter Langland's larking about has almost stopped at the moment. Today he actually brought in a book for me to read to the class, with the sections indicated by folded corners. It was not a remarkable piece of writing – some extracts from *Down with Skool* and *How to be Topp*, but it was his choice and it was a stunning success with the rest of the class. They insisted that I carry on after the lesson had ended.

Peter had a rather strange reaction to the situation. I would ask, 'What about the section on school meals?'

'Yeah. S'good.' He would reply crossly, frowning at the floor. Or, 'I dunno. 'Aven't read it,' and he would look at the wall, avoiding everyone's eyes.

About the 'nature ramble' extract, he called across to Nigel Moore.

'Listen to this un then Nig. 'S real good.'

I think the unfamiliar position of being actively and publicly in cooperation with a teacher, was a considerable strain on him. And there was some really good third-year laughter. Real stomach-clutching, diaphragm-distorting, eye-watering stuff, with no mockery or strained artificiality about it.

Only Alan Johnson was outside the effect, I think. He is an extraordinary boy, mature, intelligent, and uncompromisingly sceptical about education.

2B. At the beginning of a lesson I find Tim, whom I haven't spoken to for ages, standing in front of me.

'Hey, sir, they're lettin' us off with a reprimand.'

'Sit down. Tim, and you Lynn ...' As I absorb what he has said, I realize I must ignore the inter-lesson din.

'What was that Tim?'

'They're lettin' us off with a reprimand.'

'Who?'

'The cops, of course.'

'What is all this, Tim?'

'They said we got to go in front of the superintendent for a reprimand, but they're not going to charge us, see?'

He has a cherubic smile. He might be shyly telling me he has won a commendation card.

'Well,' I say, 'you're very lucky.' While I think to myself – what the hell's he on about. But my reply seems to have satisfied him.

'Yeah,' he says, relieved.

'Er, Tim . . .'

'Yeah?'

'What had you done?'

'Oh, bin knockin' things.'

'Knocking what?'

'Well, there's this old broken down store-house, and me 'n these other boys'd been taking things, and we got caught, see, but they said they weren't going to charge us, so we wouldn't have a record, so we could get a job later on . . . see?'

'Yeah . . . yes. But, Tim, it's serious, isn't it? I mean it's not just trouble at school, it's the law. It's one thing having teachers after you. It's quite another thing when it's the police.'

'Yeah. I know. He was a good bloke too, the one who spoke to us.'

'Right you lot! Simon, Bob, Angela, sit down . . . what on earth are you doing Lynn . . .?'

There are thirty-seven of them in the room, and the corridor over my shoulder. I must be seen to attempt to teach them all at once . . .

At the end of Jackie's last piece of writing, some instructions:

What I want on my English book
1. A critical or a complimentary comment. Not considering age, but whether another person could read it and say, 'Yes, I know what she means, this poem has some meaning.' (Somewhere!) It is something I know someone else could read without laughing themselves daft over something serious.
2. Something so that I know, in effect, if you yourself follow, dislike, understand it. Also what you think I mean.

3. Questions are good (I will grant you this point) because
they make you think more about what you have written
and help you in a way to see what the other person is
thinking.

Splendid ideas. I wish I could live up to it. But at present I am supposed to demand written work from 159 individuals every week. At five minutes a script it would take me thirteen and a quarter hours to get through. And five minutes is not enough simply to read some of them.

Half-term. A free week. And I have been painting (a) the house and (b) the plywood and frames for some new pictures. I had a lot of time for thought, and a lot of it I spent with the best of my mind analysing my discontent and my fear of school. (Schools contain a lot of fear.) Painting has been an ideal occupation; I love doing it so long as there is no real urgency to get it finished. Paint has a magic restoring effect − it re-creates old cracked yellowed surfaces it makes them cared-for. Even that dust which you are supposed to brush out from the corners, gets absorbed into the aromatic skin and becomes part of a new whole.

But by Friday I was thinking − only another standard-sized weekend to go. I felt I had only just succeeded in expanding myself again to fill my old allotment of space. Now I must once again cram myself into my diminished Grove End personality. Apologetic, ashamed, bad at the things other people there are good at, and not really wanting to be good at them. A pamphlet arrived advertising a competitive-entry exhibition, and recalled the freedom and exhilaration I felt only a year ago. But now I think . . .

'Can I do this?'

'Dare I do that?'

'How will I survive 2B?' The real heart of my fear and doubt. And then the final deadness of . . .

'Only seven weeks to go.'

'Can I live through another seven weeks?'

'What about next year?'

A constant motif emerges in the thinking. 'This situation is all wrong. Teaching is for people differently made from me.'

'At any rate,' it continues, 'teaching of this sort − with kids of this age – class – background' – until I have justified it all away and I am left with the conclusion that I am a jolly good teacher, but at present I have the wrong people to teach.

Shabby logic and shabby morality too. Yet it is this moral issue that grates ... how can it be right to assume this authoritarian mask? ... to draw oneself up on a pedagogic and chalky eminence and demand, demand, insist on ... on what? on conformity to rules of conduct I would never wish to accept myself? on acquiescence in an educational situation which is the result of a series of crazy accidents and omissions? For me it *is* a mask, a charade.

So perhaps my search for a role as a teacher ends up with my identifying that role outside all but the easiest areas where the profession operates. Top-stream fourth year – first year (at any rate for the first two terms) – my string quartet – a voluntary drama group. And, extrapolating all this into a hazy cloud-cuckoo land, I arrive again at some ideally organized liberal studies course at some ideally liberal technical college.

Shabby, shabby conclusion.

Well, well, courage – there is 2B for drama in forty minutes time. Christ! how my bowels hop at the appallingness of it – and that's no metaphor, I can feel them leaping.

Peter Langland has run away from home. The police were round at John's house at five this morning, and his friends have been grilled during second and third lessons. Members of 3A passing in the corridor say 'You won't 'ave Pete in class, today ...' or 'Pete's 'opped it, sir.' In the lesson they were all excited and laughing about it. It is a measure of the change in our relationship, that we were able after a bit to open up the seriousness of the step Peter has taken.

Nigel, for example, who claims he does not get on at all well with his parents, said he'd never run away because home was still somewhere he could go under any circumstances. Roger, who is rather spoilt at home, and who gets three times the average pocket-money of the group, and who has recently got rather involved with the semi-delinquents suddenly declared that he would run away from home if he got bad results in the exams.

'Gercha – you've got nothing to run away from.'

'Your Dad'd only say, "Now, now, Roger, you've been a naughty boy."'

In the end we agreed that things would have to be pretty rough before you would take such a step. Sorting out a cushy landing for himself before becoming committed to any dramatic gestures, Roger said he could always stay with me if he did run away. And I noticed that Nigel's knuckles are gnawed to red rawness in the unacknowledged strain under which he lives.

But Peter's disappearance was described in other terms in the staff-room.

'He's bitten off more than he can chew this time.'

'He did it on the impulse of the moment.' (His friends said he had been talking of it for some days previously.)

'He was with a group of twenty-year-olds, and they stole a car and went off to London, and Langland went with them.'

Which is the picture?

To cheer myself up, here are two things from my fourth form. I have often wondered how much poems like this first one meant to the girl who wrote them. I have been tempted to shrug them off, to assume that they are harmless posturing. I have also been tempted to take a Freudian determinist line and assume that none of it is accident, it all has meaning even if the writer didn't know it. Sally wrote this after being very depressed by the exams, and added her own detailed commentary.

Chalk, Sand and Ashes

White blossom on the falling trees,
Wailing music stirs the wind,
Dark clouds blot the sky
   And the sun never shines.

Rain constantly drumming down;
Looks, dark and heavily drawn,
Patterns printed on the wall,
   And the sun never shines.

Cold frosts stiffen the grass,
Snow blankets the crouching bulbs,
Whiteness dazzling there
  And the sun never shines.

Gloom, despair, thick like fog,
Red and blue and black
Letters flying from the pen
  And the sun never shines.

Wrinkled, ancient, small and grey
Patterns fading on the wall
The dark clouds part
  Look, see!
  The sun shines.

  And her explanation, line by line:

White blossom on the falling trees.
The attractive blossom hides the sad feeling of the tree as it
is felled. Gay clothes hide someone's feelings
underneath.

Wailing music stirs the wind
Violin music from my lesson – I HATE IT.

Dark clouds blot the sky
Incomprehensible explanations blot out the real reason
behind them.

And the sun never shines
You can't understand, 'see the light'.

Rain constantly drumming down
Hard words being said or heard

Looks, dark and heavily drawn
Frowns e.g. at the end of the day.

Patterns printed on the wall
Idea from the Paul Simon songbook. He says the pattern is
his life and the puzzle is him. A record, and I think it's
very good.

And the sun never shines
This can refer back to the 'Dark Clouds' and it provides a
link between the verses to join the poems.

Cold frosts stiffen the grass
Shocks, exams, etc. makes some people nervous and tense.

Snow blankets the crouching bulbs
The inner feelings are 'blanketed' but occasionally are
suddenly made known, 'crouching'.

Whiteness dazzling there
Literal meaning 'snow' is dazzling. I don't really
understand this line!

Gloom and despair, thick like fog
They hang over and spread around everyone, like fog.

Red and blue and black
Three predominant colours: Red – blood; blue – sad; black
– gloom.

Letters flying from the pen
I had written the poem and I could not understand it and
it seemed to me as if the pen was doing it.

Wrinkled, ancient, small and grey
Refers to old people and old things. 'Small' does not really
fit in here, I did have 'old' instead, but 'ancient' and 'old'
are not quite right.

Patterns fading on the wall
Life ending.

The dark clouds part
Two explanations: (1) at the end of life you understand
what life is all about. (2) Referring to 'dark clouds' at the
beginning, the point becomes clear and you 'see the
light'.

Look, see!
The sun shines
– everything is clear.

Well, it is still not quite clear to me! But it is a fascinating bit
of work.

Fiona, on the other hand, generally writes in crystal:

In the Groove (Or Rut as Some Call It)

I feel so good
Walking down the street
With my mod orange shoes
On my mod pinched feet.
My psychedelic paper dress
Attracts the gentlemen
(With my psychedelic stocking-tops
that show beneath the hem)
And I think I look groovy –
And swinging – and mod –
With my hair cut like a zingy
Switched-on, up-to-date Greek god.

(Why does she wears clothes that nauseate the nation?

It's all for the sake of the younger generation.)

2B. For the Tuesday lesson I simply gave them newspapers, eight between the thirty seven of them, and told them to sort out what they could about the Arab-Israeli war, then in its third day. Nearly all of them had a real go at it . . . and I thought, not for the first time, that if one could have an English room where there were always a number of things they could get on with, then one could cope better with their diversity and number.

I have been talking to Mrs Benham, the 'cello teacher, about a replacement for Michael Slater in my string quartet. I suggested Margaret in my fourth-form group, partly because I gathered she was getting fed up with music, partly because I know her a bit, and partly because she has a splendid reserved irony in her written work which interests me.

'Oh!' says Mrs Benham, 'I don't think she deserves to play quartets.'

The remark is so in keeping with the Grove End atmosphere that I don't, for a moment, take in its frightful implications.

'Why not?' I ask.

'Well, she's talented enough, but she's so damned lazy. She makes me awfully cross.'

Now it hits me.

'Well, yes, I gathered she was not getting on very well, and I thought that some playing might perhaps give her some incentive to improve.'

This idea clearly strikes Mrs Benham as offensive and unprofessional. So by way of a counter-attack she starts to praise Michael.

'Of course you'll find her very different from Michael.'

'Yes?'

'Yes. Michael, although his ear is not very good, has a first-rate brain, and is a worker. His attitude is so much better.'

Michael, I reflect, has the ideal attitude. On questions relating to feelings and opinions he has evolved a sophisticated binary language which is capable of any interpretation the hearer wishes to put on it. The elements of the language are not as crude as Yes/No, or the computer's On/Off. He answers 'I don't know' or 'I don't mind' to all questions which might involve his taking a personal stand on an issue. They are equivalent to Half on/Half off. By listening very carefully to the fractionally different tones in which he emits these signals, I have concluded that he likes playing the *Kleine Nacht Musik*, dislikes slow movements because they are dull, and dislikes fast movements because they are difficult.

On matters of fact he can be much more explicit. One day he told me that he never practised the 'cello for his lessons.

'A real worker.'

When I say, 'I don't want to be a dedicated teacher,' Anne asks, 'Who are you fooling?'

Let me explain, at least to myself. If I were more dedicated I would do more work out of school (by insisting on homework for example). I would become more of a 'schoolmaster-person'. I would have less leisure and less time for painting, for music and for reading.

Can that be a good thing? If I have any value at Grove End it must be because I stand for other ways of living than those normally opposed to the kids' ones.

It is something like this. The children are aware that they are being asked to change their way of life, their values. When they, consciously or unconsciously ask, 'What do they want me to become?' the answer must be supplied by the examples before them.

Qualities: Perseverence, idealism; self-denial; capacity to organize; a love of order.

On the debit side: moral dishonesty; narrowness; intellectual pusillanimity.

The ideal teacherly mould, as I have felt it to exist, involves one in being first a drill sergeant and then a guide, philosopher and friend. This tends to limit the example offered to the pupils, and that tends to reduce the acceptability of the example.

If I can avoid the narrowness, I might have to chuck out the perseverance, or the self-denial. Another teacher might have a fierce moral honesty which might make him bust open the orderliness of a school. So I suppose by 'dedicated' I don't just mean 'committed to teaching' but I mean 'possessing the "complete schoolmaster's" characteristics'.

Here is a pupil-eye view of what I take to be a dedicated teacher.

Here HE comes.
So up we get
Leaning against desks and muttering.
'Stand up straight!' HE yells.
People stiffen like rows of skittles.
'Sit down,' and the skittles tumble.
He complains about standards,
Issues detentions and wanders off
Onto subjects of no interest to us.
So hands fidget, doodle,
Muttering, giggling and then . . .
'Pay attention!' and skittles reappear,
Looking with unseeing eyes,
Listening with unhearing ears.
Books open, pens become active
But soon the pens hardly move,
Slowly scrawls appear on the page,
'Pens down!' and skittles again.
A pen clatters to the floor,
Murmuring giggles are soon crushed

By a stinging glare.
On HE rambles, uselessly.
HE does not realize that no one hears.
Or does HE?
Does HE know what HE'S on about?
HE looks over his book. At what?
At people or statues?
HE turns to the blackboard
A paper dart flies and crashes,
A bottle of ink is spilt.
HE turns, and is greeted
With a feeble excuse which HE accepts.
How much longer can this last?
HE explains HIS diagram.
To whom? To HIMSELF perhaps?
To the skittles now slouched in chairs?
   Suddenly it happens . . .
It rings and life comes to the room.
Books crammed into satchels
Tear out of the room,
'For homework tonight . . .'
But everyone is gone.
The battle is fought,
HE is alone on the battlefield,
   Just HIM.

1. Is that a model we would like them to adopt?
2. What chance is there of them adopting it anyway?

Reading through and thinking through this diary, now that my probationary year is very nearly past, I find I have been too kind to myself in some ways. I have intermittently confessed to inefficiency and lack of discipline, but at the same time I have been saying 'so what?' They were appeals which ask, 'are these things as sacred as my colleagues would have me think?' After the event I see that I never really disapproved of what I had done or thought. Even when I have quite honestly accused myself of failure, I have not taken the blame for it – I have managed to shift it onto the school, or the system, or something.

But there have been occasions when I have failed in my own eyes, and they are not in the diary. Should they be?

Here is one from a safe six months ago. I can remember one of those awful Monday 2B lessons shortly before Christmas, when with a divided self that would not reunite I was unforgivably and uselessly hurling abuse at them. They took no notice. Mr Peters, the new senior master, was trying to teach a sixth-form group in his room across the corridor and since he could not hear himself, or his pupils, he decided he had better intervene. The room was a shambles of singing, fighting, laughing and talking. I was right at the back remonstrating with two boys who were playing table football. And I was wishing the twenty-five minutes to go before my release would shrink to twenty seconds.

It was only that *his* 'Mr Otty', at my elbow, was in a basso unattainable by a second former, that made me look up sweating and sinking internally. (I'll say this for 2B, they had continued their performance uninterrupted by Mr Peters's presence.)

'I wonder, Mr Otty, if you could quieten this lot down a bit? I'm trying to . . .'

'Oh, certainly, Mr Peters. I'm so sorry. I'd no idea I was . . .'

On his departure, with a kind of desperate honesty, I said something like 'Now look what you've done.' A very small boy whose face was somewhere down by my right hip made some apt and confidently cheeky retort, which caused rage to surge from deep inside me. My right arm, moved to violence, came up sharply, almost involuntarily, I remember, to clout him on the back of the head. And years of restraint and disapproval tangled the muscles, slowed the blow, and deflected it to a glancing cuff that hardly ruffled his hair, but fear and surprise made his face rumple and redden into tears. My guts turned in self-hate and fear that made me laugh protectively and try to shrug it off.

The children were not deceived. Anne's forthright condemnation still makes my ears tingle. Although the incident has hovered vivid in my mind I have never really looked at it until now.

I have a curious feeling of defeat about teaching – not just my teaching – the whole profession. There is, I suppose, the contrast between Grove End's squalor, and counsel's chambers, where the intellectual jungle is actualized in hard cash, and carpets, and a shape on the map of London, and a position in the world. People I know in other professions can make me feel singularly small and shapeless, or else foolishly missionary and dedicated, as though I had taken a morally right, but socially perverse option with my life.

Then there is my perception of the task. I share with my colleagues the desire to alter the attitudes of the children. I would, for example, like them to approach new experience in literature and art and so on, with a live curiosity, rather than the deadly rejection syndrome which is typical of Grove End. I am depressed by the automatic first response of so many of the children.

'Aw, not ...' (Not what? poetry, pictures, reading, writing, music, discussion, an idea.) Now some people I know can get morally righteous in this situation. They can condemn the reaction with 'oughts' and 'ought nots', and this gives them impetus to carry on what they see as the battle. But I get sick at heart as I enumerate feebly and defeatedly the irremovable conditions of the children's lives both in and out of school, which seem to me to make their attitudes inevitable.

And then there is the whole situation in which the education takes place. The structure from top to bottom is shored up by the acceptance by those in it of what is offered by those above them. Since this produces situations which are so unsuitable for the achievement of the declared aims and ends of education, how can one expect anything but rejection from the children. *We* still accept classes of nearer forty than twenty, and classrooms that are an affront to the spirit, and a staffroom that ought to be an offence. We may accept for high motives – but the disadvantages of acceptance are clearer than the motives. The children want to be different from us defeated-looking objects with our limited gestures, and our apparently minimal demands on life. Unfortunately to become different they reject what we so feebly stand for; art, literature, mental discipline, selflessness.

Each year at the school dedication service, we pray that the truth may be fearlessly sought out and fearlessly proclaimed!

Afterwards

As my probationary year recedes into the past, there is less, not more, that I want to put into this diary. Things have not got suddenly or spectacularly better, but they grind less. I have not magically mastered the trick of discipline, and I still feel very isolated. But I think that it must be that last year and the year before I was writing in order to shape a root structure that would let me go on teaching and yet remain me, myself. I think this means that I will always have difficulty persuading a class to sit down, or to be quiet, or whatever. It is almost as though the compulsory framework of a school made the child's reaction to compulsion one of the central elements in the teacher–pupil relationship. If my own mind were not so divided in its reaction to the compulsory element it would, I think, be easier; the children would be able to take that issue as settled, as not worth working over with me. I think that's how some teachers are happy in this school. They feel in accord with the institutional framework (even if they criticize the details). I don't. And I can't see that I ever will here. But having got that fact clear, it is easier than it was.

After all that sweat and blood and tears, 2B, almost without exception, became my best friends at Grove End. As soon as I stopped teaching them, they started bringing me their writing to read, asking me about their problems, telling me what was happening to them in their progress up the school. As an example of what I mean, here is a piece written by Lynn (crazy, noisy, angry, rude, sulky Lynn), two days after the end of the summer term.

What I am doing at this moment

The time is 1.30 a.m. in the middle of the night, and I just can't sleep. Do you ever get nights when you just can't sleep? I've got hay fever, I'm boiling hot, and my nose is running. (I haven't got a handkerchief on me.) Everything is silent. All I can hear is one or two cars on the distant main road.

What made me write a composition? I don't know, but I just had a feeling I wanted to. I suppose this will be the last essay I write for you, Mr Otty, this year, but I do hope you teach me another time. I am really sorry if I was badly behaved at any times, because when I think about the last three terms I wasn't an exceptionally well disciplined member of the form, was I?

I expect when you read this you'll think I'm mad, but I can quite assure you I am normal. I just feel like writing. By the way, I mean to write a book. But knowing me I will start it, become bored and abandon an unfinished masterpiece. When I was small (not so many years ago) I remember reading a book by a twelve year old . . . about John going to the park to meet two swans . . . so if that can be published, mine should. I doubt if I will even finish a chapter though.

I wonder what you are doing at this moment. (Not the moment you read it, but tonight, Friday 21st.) Anyway, I suppose I'd better go to sleep. It will be back to the hard labour now we haven't got you for a teacher.

Good night.

It is the certainty that all will be forgiven that amazes me! And of course ensures that all is forgiven.

I no longer believe in the persuasive power of sweet reason. Almost exactly a year to the day after the staff meeting which nearly drove me from teaching, we have had another one on the same subject of letting the children use their classrooms at lunch and break. With almost no discussion it was agreed that this was a good idea. I kept my mouth shut, so I can claim no credit for the change. The arguments for and against were the same last year – the atmosphere must have been different. The only person who spoke against the idea was old Ernest Hopkins. He has such a powerful belief in original sin.

'You've just got to face it,' he said, 'children *are* destructive and they've got to be restrained until they grow out of it.'

Well there is a lot of evidence which could be on his side. Why, for example, is every desk in Grove End the object of a continued attack on its fabric? Why are the screws worked out of the desk-lids with such an agony of furtive concentration? Why are the asbestos panels in the walls kicked in, and the hole enlarged with delighted excitement? I would almost bet that every pupil at

Grove End has had a go, at one time or another, at these activities.

All that is so and yet I'm still convinced that Hopkins's way makes matters worse, and he's convinced that anything else is naïve weakness. There is no arguing from 'is' to 'ought'.

Peter Langland did return to Grove End after his runaway episode, but only for a short time. The tone in which he was discussed in staff meetings suddenly changed; from being a 'rogue' he became a 'psychiatric case' ... snap ... just like that. Then he threatened a teacher with a knife, and vanished. At the meeting where we were told he had been suspended, and was now to go to a special boarding school, we were also told we must pay no attention so that the kids should not find out.

As soon as I met some of 3A – now fourth formers and starting the exam grind – it was:

'Where's Pete Langland, sir?'

'I 'eard 'e's in 'ospital. Is that right, sir?'

'No. Alan saw 'im the other night. He says 'e's been given the boot.'

'P'raps he's run away again, pinched a car ... where'll they find him this time? He's a case isn't he, sir!'

To halt some of this riotous speculation I tell them as much of the truth as I know.

It is so sad, last year a whacking was often recommended. It would knock some sense into him. Now we can wash our hands of him and declare that we knew all along he was unstable. As long as there is a label which decently hides the obscure reality of a human child, then it doesn't matter how suddenly and irrationally we swap the labels about.

Why didn't I say a word at the staff meeting?

1. What would be the point? I still have not recovered from my last attempt at public debate.

2. Anyway, secretly I am still vulnerable enough to be relieved that he is no longer around to embarrass me by calling loudly in front of other teachers,

'Oi, sir, goin' up Grove Hill?'

'Yes, at five o'clock.'

'Give us a lift.'

'O.K. See you at the car at five.'

(He never turned up!)

Or again in the corridor:

' 'Ello, NICK,' grotesque kissing gesture, smacking of distorted lips, ' 'Ere a minute ... got a fag for oi? Go on, I'm dying for a drag.'

'Don't be a clot, Pete,' I'd say, prickling with angst.

3. Because I don't teach him this year, and I know in spite of all I would like to think, what a relief it was when he was absent from my lessons last year (knocking off – having a fag in the bogs – I didn't care a damn – I was free of him).

4. It was too late anyway for *our* school to do anything for him. How could the staff and he have confidence in one another now?

If only we could have the courage and imagination to see that it is not what a kid is, but how we can relate to it that really matters. A consciously adopted repulsiveness demands to be loved, and no other response has a hope of achieving anything. I wonder what his future holds. I am afraid that the more institutional it is, the more disastrous it will be.

I can't get some things out of my mind. 'An air raid' was the topic of one composition last year. Peter's contribution was weird. A spider's web of bold but disturbed draughtsmanship (see next page). Off centre in it a rudimentary spider, a scribbled biro blob and eight little hooked legs. Above this picture was the composition:

If we were in a war and in an air raid I'd change myself to spider-man and make a strong web to catch all the bombs that fell.

An air raid

If we were in a war and in
an air raid I'd change myself
to Spider man and make a strong
web to catch all the bombs that
fell.

I almost tore it up, it was so scruffy and short, but it grows on you. It is full of a touching protectiveness towards his fellow humans.

What I don't understand is that Mr Curle seems to approve of me now. After a fantastic series of charades including letters of application and references and even interviews surrounded with dark webs of intrigue, he has decided to promote me to second in the English department, and to give me an allowance from next September. I cannot see what I have done to recommend myself to him. He still peers through the corridor window and makes my heart stop at the thought of what he must be seeing. Perhaps it is my public-school and Oxbridge background. Perhaps it is that I have not said 'Yessir,' but have ground on at my own way of doing things. But as the news has spread it has helped my situation in the staff-room. I even find myself befriended by and friendly towards Richard Davies, the bearded gwg, who berated me a year ago about 'free-expression lessons'.

Perhaps people just think that I'm not going away, and I'm not going to change, and therefore they might as well accommodate me somehow.

Finally a piece written by one of 2B much later, when he was in the fifth form and a friend of his was being vigorously 'advised out' of the school.

I very often wonder why teachers should have so much power over us. They have the power to tell us what we should wear, how long we should have our hair, and they are even able to smash people into blubbering wrecks with the threat of expulsion.

The whole point of schools seems to be to breed robots, computerized idiots whose only thoughts are those of their immediate superiors. They do not encourage individual thought, but force upon people conformist attitudes and points of view.

Unless you hit out against it you become robotic images of parents and teachers. If you do hit out against it you are accused of being an anarchist, told you are stupid and a bad influence on others.

I am totally against this system and have shown it in various ways since I have been at this school. My hair is long because I like long hair, and I intend to keep it that way. Unhappily the reason why I do not wear school uniform is not that I am deliberately breaking school rules, but that I cannot wear it for various reasons.

(He is one of a family of six; they can't afford to spend money on uniform just for the last few months of his fifth year.)

We are told that teachers are superior to us, but in what way? I expect that a lot more serious thought goes on in my head than in quite a number of teachers' heads, though it might be in different fields.

Myself, I would not like to tell teachers what to do. I would like for them to listen to and respect my point of view as I like to think I respect theirs.